Federal Civilian Workforce Hiring, Recruitment, and Related Compensation Practices for the Twenty-First Century

Review of Federal HR Demonstration Projects and
Alternative Personnel Systems to Identify Best
Practices and Lessons Learned

GINGER GROEBER, PAUL W. MAYBERRY, BRANDON CROSBY,
MARK DOBOGA, SAMANTHA E. DINICOLA, CAITLIN LEE,
ELLEN E. TUNSTALL

Prepared for the Office of the Secretary of Defense
Approved for public release; distribution unlimited

NATIONAL DEFENSE RESEARCH INSTITUTE

For more information on this publication, visit www.rand.org/t/RR3168

Library of Congress Cataloging-in-Publication Data is available for this publication.
ISBN: 978-1-9774-0378-0

Published by the RAND Corporation, Santa Monica, Calif.
© Copyright 2020 RAND Corporation
RAND® is a registered trademark.

Support RAND
Make a tax-deductible charitable contribution at
www.rand.org/giving/contribute

www.rand.org

Preface

The U.S. federal government—the single largest direct-hiring organization in the nation—employs around 2 million civilian personnel. The authority to hire and manage civilians is covered by a patchwork of human capital programs and rules, primarily under Titles 5, 10, 32, and 38 of the U.S. Code. Over time, this broad collection of authorities has failed to keep pace with the dynamics of the current workforce and has also resulted in a range of workforce inequities. In an attempt to address such systemic problems, the federal government has implemented a variety of incremental changes over the years. The reforms have targeted select agencies and job types and created an intricate system of demonstration projects, alternative personnel systems (APSs), and direct-hire authorities.

While providing additional flexibilities to certain agencies, these reforms have often resulted in multiple human resources (HR) systems and even greater complexities. A number of other real-time factors are also affecting federal personnel management: high demand for science and technology workers, competition with the private sector, requirements for U.S. citizenship, security clearances, and the aging of the current workforce. Accordingly, the President's Management Agenda (PMA) has focused on creating a modern workforce that aligns staff skills with evolving federal mission needs in the context of today's competitive work environment.

One goal within the PMA focuses on developing a workforce for the twenty-first century, with a subgoal associated with simple and strategic hiring. Associated with this goal and to inform efforts to improve hiring practices, the Department of Defense (DoD) was tasked with providing an overview of the array of HR demonstration projects and APSs put in place throughout the federal government over the past decade in order to identify promising practices for consideration in federal HR reform efforts. The objective of this study was to assist DoD in responding to this tasking.

To accomplish this, the study team compiled a list of HR demonstration projects, APSs, and direct-hire authorities across the federal government. Our inquiry focused on programs for recruiting, hiring, and related compensation aspects instituted since 2008; the timing of the government's last major report on these topics; and the identification of potential effective practices employed by these programs. In the conduct of assessment of effective practices, the study team also identified a number of evaluation process and implementation shortfalls. In this area the report offers general observations and possible considerations that DoD and other federal agencies may explore further. The research reported here was completed in August 2019 and underwent security review with the sponsor and the Defense Office of Prepublication and Security Review before public release.

This research was sponsored by the Deputy Assistant Secretary of Defense for Civilian Personnel Policy and conducted within the Forces and Resources Policy Center of the RAND National Defense Research Institute, a federally funded research and development center sponsored by the Office of the Secretary of Defense, the Joint Staff, the Unified Combatant Commands, the U.S. Marine Corps, the U.S. Navy, the defense agencies, and the defense Intelligence Community.

For more information on the RAND Forces and Resources Policy Center, see www.rand.org/nsrd/ndri/centers/frp or contact the director (contact information is provided on the webpage).

Contents

Tables

Summary

Historically, the federal human resources (HR) system originated from processes put in place under the Pendleton Act of 1885. Over time, this act evolved and gradually developed into over 6,000 pages of civil service laws, procedures, and regulations. In 1978, the Civil Service Reform Act was passed to modernize HR systems and to focus on pay-for-performance practices and improving the recruitment and retention of federal employees. The act also authorized the Office of Personnel Management (OPM) to work with federal agencies in developing and overseeing demonstration projects intended to implement and assess improved federal HR management methods and technologies. Beginning in 1980, the OPM could authorize and assess up to ten such demonstration projects at any given time within certain parameters. Many of these projects featured innovations in recruiting and hiring practices. Because of the limitations on demonstration projects, federal agencies also pursued flexibilities through direct congressional authorization to establish alternative personnel systems (APSs). Likewise, based on a persistent inability of agencies to fill vacancies for critical hiring needs and severe shortages of qualified candidates, direct-hire authorities (DHAs) were also instituted in the early 2000s.

The 2018 President's Management Agenda (PMA) continues this reform progression and provides a long-term vision for modernizing the federal government in key areas. The PMA identifies cross-agency priorities (CAPs), which are goals that target areas where multiple agencies can collaborate to effect change and report progress. These efforts are being pursued to align and strategically manage the workforce to efficiently and effectively achieve the federal government mission.

One of the PMA CAP goals is to develop a workforce for the twenty-first century, which includes subgoal 3, Enabling Simple and Strategic Hiring Practices.[1] To help the federal government achieve this subgoal, DoD was tasked with the responsibility of examining best practices of federal demonstration projects and APSs. The Office of the Deputy Assistant Secretary of Defense for Civilian Personnel Policy, or DASD(CPP), is responsible for addressing the PMA CAP subgoal 3 and asked the RAND Corporation to support its efforts. In particular, DASD(CPP) asked RAND to identify best practices and lessons for recruiting, hiring, and related aspects of compensation in demonstration projects and APSs that could offer solutions for federal agencies seeking to streamline their existing practices and improve their ability to recruit and retain top talent.

Scope and Approach

After discussions with key civilian personnel stakeholders and guidance from the sponsor, the scope of our analysis was limited to flexible practices related to hiring and recruiting civilian members of the federal workforce, as well as associated compensation matters. The time period for our analysis was January 2008–May 2019 and included programs from agencies of sufficient size. This resulted in a listing of 20 demonstration projects, 21 APSs, and six DHAs.

Our study results were informed by multiple data sources analyzed via multiple methods. We conducted a literature review and initial analysis to understand the historical context of current and past demonstration projects, APSs, and DHAs within the scope of our study. This review encompassed legislation that authorized and modified projects, including government reports, articles, and scholarly papers. We augmented the literature review with an initial series of interviews with civilian HR representatives from military departments

---

[1] PMA, "Workforce for the 21st Century," webpage, undated.

and intelligence and acquisition communities to gain broad perspectives of policy justifications for past programs.

For the identified list of demonstration projects, APSs, and DHAs, we sought to collect definitive documentation of evaluations conducted for relevant HR flexibilities that were implemented. Such publicly accessible evaluations were available for only eight programs. Accordingly, we conducted a second series of structured interviews with HR professionals across the federal government associated with the above-referenced projects to gather information on successful practices, documented program outcomes, and features of the systems that stood out as potential effective practices.

We employed an approach that divided practices into three effectiveness categories based on the veracity of study design and analysis, rigor of available data, and replication of findings:

- Best practices: evidence-based replicated practices proven to aid multiple organizations reach high levels of efficiency or effectiveness.
- Promising practices: practices that have been shown to work effectively and produce successful outcomes but replicated on a limited scale. These practices are supported to varying degrees by objective and subjective data, but not validated with the same rigor as best practices.
- Innovative practices: practices that have worked within one organization and show early promise for progressing to more demonstrated impact.

During our analysis, we also discovered a number of evaluation process and implementation shortfalls. Although we did not explicitly set out to identify such issues, a number of topics consistently arose during our discussions. The sponsor expressed interest in understanding these process and implementation shortfalls so that DoD (and potentially the OPM and the broader federal HR community) could consider them in a more comprehensive context associated with their emphasis on continuous process improvement.

Effective Practices

We applied our effective practice methodology to the population of practices implemented across agencies and organized the results in three categories: recruiting, hiring, and related aspects of compensation reform. The effective practices identified are listed by category in Table S.1, along with the practice type.

According to our interviews with federal HR professionals, these practices have helped reduce the duration of vacancies, increased access to applicants, helped identify candidates for hard-to-fill positions, facilitated on-the-spot job offers at recruiting events, and allowed for noncompetitive hiring, as well as other benefits. In particular, use of DHAs and compensation effective practices have helped attract candidates for scientific and technology positions where competition with the civilian workplace is keen. Compensation effective practices, such as the contribution-based compensation and appraisal system, can also have a positive effect on retention by benefiting top performers in an organization. And some effective practices, such as the three-year probationary period, have helped ensure that candidates are in fact the best match for a particular job, the best qualified applicants are being considered, and top performers are retained.

Considerations for Improving Assessment and Dissemination of Effective Practices

Our systematic review of program practices resulted in a secondary outcome of interest to the project sponsor—issues associated with specification, conduct, oversight, and reporting of the evaluation process and implementation shortfalls. We provide these observations and considerations for DoD's further exploration.

Specifying evaluation standards. We learned from our interviews that the OPM is not currently engaged in either conducting or overseeing program evaluations, nor has any other body filled this void. Interviewees emphasized that with no such requirements, most agencies do not engage in systematic efforts to collect and share data on

Table S.1
Identification and Categorization of Effective Practices

Category	Effective Practice	Practice Type
Recruiting	• Interagency collaborations (e.g., collaborative job announcements and applicant sourcing for like positions among different agencies)	Innovative
	• Video interviewing	Innovative
	• Aggressive outreach and DHAs (e.g., making job offers at recruiting events)	Promising
	• Student employment programs (e.g., job fair outreach and postdoctoral fellowship programs)	Innovative
Hiring	• Direct-hire authorities managed by organization, not external authorities	Best
	• A three-year probationary period to allow supervisors to make permanent hiring decisions based on employees' demonstrated capabilities	Best
	• Modified veterans' preference	Promising
	• Student hires placed in more general positions and then advanced to long-term assignments as positions open	Innovative
Compensation	• Pay bands that provide flexibility in placement and discussions with candidates on upward mobility	Best
	• A contribution-based compensation and appraisal system	Best
	• Advancing in-hire rates without prior approval	Promising
	• Checks and balances in the performance management and payout processes to ensure fair treatment of all employees	Best

program outcomes. Interviewees also noted lack of program account-ability, inability to assess the need for program modification, and lack of essential information to inform agency leadership in decisionmak-ing processes. One way to reenergize today's stagnant evaluation pro-cess would be to establish a forum where interagency representatives can collaborate in identifying a uniform set of evaluative data and stan-dards to be collected and analyzed for every program. It will be neces-sary to account for differences in project design and innovations being pursued and accordingly build in sufficient flexibility. Evaluation and data specifications outlined in the fiscal year 2019 National Defense Authorization Act may assist in development of uniform guidelines. To facilitate retention of evaluation outcomes, we believe that a successful approach would be to establish a publicly available central repository. All agencies could contribute data and have access to the information for each program so they could share and learn from the posted prac-tices and effectiveness determinations.

Determining and implementing effective practices. Based on our interviews and literature review, the study team found no evidence of government- or agency-wide standards for identifying effective HR practices that might become candidates for implementation across the government. We also learned that there was no requirement for agen-cies to systematically consider practice outcomes of other agencies as they sought to design and implement appropriate flexibilities for their own workforce. We offer that an interagency forum should consider developing standards for determining effective practices. The method and criteria applied in the present study could serve as a starting point. This forum could also establish and implement an appropriate mecha-nism through which effective practices and outcomes would routinely be examined for broader adaption by other agencies. Such a forum should be based on existing executive governance bodies, executed as an ongoing requirement and focus area, and augmented by functional expertise or other process stakeholders on an as-needed basis. The 14 effective practices identified in this study could serve as a starting point for this interagency mechanism and then allow individual agencies to conduct the necessary due diligence to determine applicability to their circumstances.

Overcoming roadblocks to HR change. Our interviewees reported a number of obstacles to establishing agency-level reforms, but two impediments were raised repeatedly. First, agencies must devote substantial time and resources to execute significant HR change. New authorities may take years to implement, which is often at odds with leadership emphasis to achieve "quick wins." If agencies budget for the necessary time to research effective practices and ensure that sufficient resources are available to support the workload required for design, implementation, and evaluation, we believe that HR staffs would be more likely to pursue effective flexibilities. In this manner agencies may be more likely to consider successful HR programs and apply appropriately tailored practices to support their agency missions and strategic needs (which may possibly achieve some economies). Second, most demonstration projects do not cover union employees. Agency HR professionals explained that it takes considerable time for union employees to transition into such programs—that is, if they ever do. The innovative approach successfully implemented by the Air Force Research Laboratory may provide agencies and union personnel with a degree of flexibility to address both organizational needs and individual preferences. Such successes may lead to insights on how to engage positively with unions to participate in program justification, design, implementation, and ultimately participation on the part of its members.

Reducing HR system complexity. We found through our literature review that personnel systems have continued to proliferate across the federal government in recent years. Our interviews confirmed this finding, with HR professionals emphasizing that such proliferation results in complexity, making it difficult to understand and stay abreast of recruiting, hiring, and related compensation legislative and policy options, thereby increasing the likelihood for implementation errors. We offer several considerations related to consolidating DHAs, assessing requirements for public notice in job announcements, and evaluating gaps in available training for HR professionals and managers.

Conclusion

The findings and observations in this report can inform the government's direction as it addresses the need for a talented and high-performing workforce supported by contemporary and effective HR systems and practices. These considerations can be critical to modernizing and refining current personnel programs, as well to the design and implementation of programs for new organizations, such as a merged DoD commissary and exchange organization and the U.S. Space Corps. The considerations also support DoD and the OPM in achieving CAP subgoal 3, developing a workforce for the twenty-first century.

Acknowledgments

We are grateful to the many people who were involved in this research. In particular, we thank our sponsor, Veronica Hinton, principal director, ODASD(CPP), for her help and guidance throughout this study; she was very gracious with her time, expertise, and professional advice. At the Defense Civilian Personnel Advisory Service, Daniel Hester, who serves as the deputy director, and Jeff Nelson, the technical director, provided insights and feedback at each of our project reviews and for the final report.

We also acknowledge the data and interviews provided by individuals in many defense organizations and other federal agencies. Pivotal roles were played by leaders in the following organizations and programs: the Acquisition Workforce Demonstration Project, the Agricultural Research Service, the Air Force Research Laboratory Demonstration Project, the Defense Civilian Intelligence Personnel System, the Department of Homeland Security, the National Credit Union Administration, the Office of the Comptroller of the Currency, the National Institute of Standards and Technology, the National Nuclear Security Administration, the National Security Agency, Navy Demonstration Projects, the Office of Personnel Management, the Office of the Under Secretary of Defense for Intelligence, and the Department of Veterans Affairs.

This research benefited from helpful insights and comments provided by several RAND colleagues, including Craig Bond, Susan Gates, Lisa Harrington, and John Winkler, and by the external review conducted by Jim Green. Their thoughtful comments greatly improved this report. We also thank Barbara Bicksler for her contributions to making this study concise and consistent in its messaging.

Abbreviations

5 C.F.R.	Title 5 of the Code of Federal Regulations
5 U.S.C.	Title 5 of the U.S. Code
AcqDemo	Acquisition Workforce Demonstration Project
AFRL	Air Force Research Laboratory
APS	alternative personnel system
ARS	Agriculture Research Service
CAP	cross-agency priority
CAPS	Commerce Alternative Personnel System
CCAS	Contribution-Based Compensation and Appraisal System
CES	Cyber Excepted Service
CFPB	Consumer Financial Protection Bureau
CSRA	Civil Service Reform Act
DASD(CPP)	Deputy Assistant Secretary of Defense for Civilian Personnel Policy
DCIPS	Defense Civilian Intelligence Personnel System
DHA	direct-hire authority
DHS	Department of Homeland Security
DoC	Department of Commerce
DoD	Department of Defense
DoE	Department of Energy
DoT	Department of Transportation
FAA	Federal Aviation Administration
FEVS	Federal Employee Viewpoint Survey

FIRREA	Financial Institutions Reform, Recovery, and Enforcement Act of 1989
FRN	Federal Register Notice
FY	fiscal year
GAO	Government Accountability Office
GS	General Schedule
HR	human resources
IC	intelligence community
IRS	Internal Revenue Service
Lab Demo	Laboratory Demonstration Project
NAVSEA	Naval Sea Systems Command
NAPA	National Academy of Public Administration
NCUA	National Credit Union Administration
NDAA	National Defense Authorization Act
NGA	National Geospatial-Intelligence Agency
NIST	National Institute of Standards and Technology
NNSA	National Nuclear Security Administration
NSA	National Security Agency
NSPS	National Security Personnel System
OCC	Office of the Comptroller of the Currency
OPM	Office of Personnel Management
PASS	Performance Accountability and Standards System
PM PRA	Performance Management Performance Review Authority
PMA	President's Management Agenda
STEM	science, technology, engineering, and mathematics
STRL	Science and Technology Reinvention Laboratory
TIGTA	Treasury Inspector General for Tax Administration
TSA	Transportation Security Administration
U.S.C.	United States Code
USDA	U.S. Department of Agriculture
VA	Department of Veterans Affairs

CHAPTER ONE

Introduction

As the single largest direct employer in the nation, the U.S. federal government employs around 2 million civilian personnel nationwide.[1] Today the provisions of Title 5 of the United States Code (5 U.S.C.) cover the majority of federal workers and specify federal human resources (HR) practices for most government agencies. Human capital experts, federal employees, and the current administration have warned that the federal civilian HR system, first established in the nineteenth century, is failing to keep pace with the dynamics of the twenty-first-century workforce.[2]

Although the nature of the work performed by federal employees has changed, the HR system has remained anchored in the era of high-volume paper processes and lower-graded administrative support staffs. Staffing the enterprise, specifically the Department of Defense (DoD) Science and Technology Reinvention Laboratories (STRLs), is complicated by factors such as the high demand for science and technology workers, competition with the private sector, the requirement for U.S. citizenship, the need for new hires to obtain security clearances,

---

[1] OPM, "Executive Branch Civilian Employment Since 1940," 2014.

[2] Federal employees and managers noted in a 2017 OPM survey that the system fails to reward the best and address the worst employees. See OPM, *Federal Employee Viewpoint Survey: Governmentwide Management Report*, Washington, D.C.: U.S. Office of Personnel Management, 2017b. For OPM views of problems with civilian personnel management, see, for example, OPM, *End to End Hiring Initiative*, Washington, D.C.: U.S. Office of Personnel Management, March 2017a, p. 4.

and the aging of the federal workforce.[3] Reflecting years of concern, the President's Management Agenda (PMA) named hiring and firing as two major components of a twenty-first-century workforce priority goal, calling the current 5 U.S.C. HR system "a relic of an earlier era."[4]

Recruiting, hiring, and aspects of compensation related to these activities are areas of concern across the federal government. In 2017, the U.S. Office of Personnel Management (OPM) noted that over the next five years the federal government expected to lose "a significant portion of its workforce" due to retirement.[5] It is critical for the government to recruit and hire high-caliber applicants to replace these employees to ensure the efficient and effective management of critical governmental programs. Yet a 2017 Federal Employee Viewpoint Survey (FEVS) found that only 32 percent of federal employees believed their work unit was able to recruit people with the right skills; that percentage marked a decrease from 2016. While the 2018 survey numbers released during the present study indicate an increase to 42 percent, this item remains one of the lowest areas of agreement.[6]

For years, federal managers have complained that federal hiring procedures—particularly those associated with the most commonly used hiring authority, "competitive examining"[7]—were rigid and complex. Managers have often expressed the need for more flexibility

---

[3] U.S. Government Accountability Office (GAO), *Further Actions Needed to Strengthen Oversight and Coordination of Defense Laboratories' Hiring Efforts*, Washington, D.C.: U.S. Government Accountability Office, GAO 18-417, May 2018.

[4] OMB, *President's Management Agenda: Modernizing Government for the 21st Century*, Washington, D.C.: U.S. Office of Management and Budget, March 20, 2018, p. 3.

[5] OPM, 2017a, p. 4.

[6] OPM, 2017b, pp. 3–5; OPM, *Federal Employee Viewpoint Survey: Governmentwide Management Report*, Washington, D.C.: U.S. Office of Personnel Management, 2018, p. 5.

[7] Title 5 of the Code of Federal Regulations (5 C.F.R.), Part 332, Recruitment and Selection through Competitive Examination, outlines OPM regulations with the traditional method for making appointments to the competitive service positions and requires adherence to 5 U.S.C. competitive examining requirements.

within a system that has traditionally been based on a "one-size-fits-all" approach with uniform rules across government set forth in 5 U.S.C.[8]

Because federal agencies may need flexibilities not available in 5 U.S.C., some HR reforms have been approved and implemented for select agencies and job types. Because these reforms are not available for all agencies or job types, they exist alongside the general hiring authorities and thus create a system of new hiring authorities and alternative personnel systems (APSs) so complicated that few hiring managers understand the intricacies of available authorities within their agencies.[9] As a result, it is difficult for agencies to take full advantage of flexibilities that might improve their hiring outcomes. In 2016, for example, the GAO reported that federal agencies were using relatively few of their available hiring authorities and that OPM officials did not know whether this was because agencies are "unfamiliar with other authorities, of if they have found other authorities to be less effective."[10]

Given the complexity of the federal hiring authorities, the 2018 PMA calls on the administration to work with the U.S. Congress to update and streamline the federal government's personnel management system.[11] One of the PMA cross-agency priority (CAP) goals is to develop a workforce for the twenty-first century, which includes subgoal 3, Enabling Simple and Strategic Hiring Practices.[12] To help the federal government achieve this subgoal, the DoD was tasked with

---

[8] GAO, *Human Capital: Effective Use of Flexibilities Can Assist Agencies in Managing Their Workforces*, Washington, D.C.: U.S. Government Accountability Office, GAO-03-2, December 6, 2002.

[9] Eric Katz, "How Attempts at Fixing the Civil Service System Have Made It Worse Off," *Government Executive*, October 10, 2018.

[10] According to the GAO report, "Of the 105 hiring authorities used in fiscal year 2014, agencies relied on 20 for 91 percent of the 196,226 new appointments made that year." See GAO, *Federal Hiring: OPM Needs to Improve Management and Oversight of Hiring Authorities*, Washington, D.C.: U.S. Government Accountability Office, GAO-16-521, August 2016.

[11] OPM, *President's Management Agenda: Modernizing Government for the 21st Century*, Washington, D.C.: U.S. Office of Management and Budget, March 20, 2018.

[12] PMA, undated.

the responsibility of examining best practices of federal demonstration projects and APSs. This report aims to assist the Office of the Deputy Assistant Secretary of Defense for Civilian Personnel Policy, or DASD(CPP), in meeting this requirement.

Research Scope and Limitations

DoD asked the RAND Corporation to identify potential best practices and lessons for recruiting, hiring, and related compensation that could offer new solutions for federal agencies seeking to streamline their existing practices with the aim of improving their ability to recruit and retain top talent. Based on initial engagement of the study team with select key civilian personnel stakeholders and additional guidance from the sponsor after commissioning of the study, we refined—with sponsor concurrence—the precise tasking to account for both the quality and availability of evaluative data. The following scope and analytical limitations resulted from these discussions.

First, the study focused on demonstration projects and APSs approved by Congress or the OPM since the passage of the Civil Service Reform Act (CSRA), codified in 5 U.S.C., in 1978. While the PMA CAP subgoal calls for strategies that make it easier to recruit top talent, reduce the hiring cycle timeline, and improve applicant assessment, DASD(CPP) asked RAND to limit its assessment of flexible practices to those related to hiring and recruiting of civilians in the federal workforce that were active as of May 2019 or put in place since 2008.[13]

Thus, our analysis focused on 40 demonstration projects and APSs that met these conditions. This included several programs that had evolved from a demonstration project to an APS, but it excluded three programs put in place prior to 2008 that had been terminated:

[13] The year 2008 was selected by the sponsor because this period was just before the OPM released its last report summarizing these activities. See OPM, *Alternative Personnel Systems in the Federal Government: A Status Report on Demonstration Projects and Other Performance-Based Pay Systems*, Washington, D.C.: U.S. Office of Personnel Management, December 2007.

the DoD National Security Personnel System (NSPS); an APS at the Bureau of Alcohol, Tobacco, Firearms and Explosives within the Department of Justice; and a demonstration project at the Alcohol and Tobacco Tax and Trade Bureau within the Department of the Treasury. The sponsor explicitly did not want a reconsideration of the NSPS, though in Chapter Two we provide an overview and characterize several union-related issues and concerns that contributed to its termination.

Second, the study team also limited its review to agencies with employee populations of more than 2,000 (excluding those agencies listed in the 2008 report) because their flexibilities would have limited relationship to larger more complex agencies in the federal government and likely have limited application to DoD. The study team also did not include any quasi-governmental agencies.

Third, we employed an approach that broadens the identification of "best" practices. To the extent that evaluative studies and findings are available for government programs, we conducted the evidence-based and comparative analysis necessary to accurately and confidently make valid determinations of best practices. To the extent that such information does not exist, is not available, or is not of sufficient quality, we conducted alternative analyses based on supplementary data and interviews with HR professionals. Such alternative analyses resulted in practices that cannot be categorized as "best" based on a paucity of information or limits in analytical power to make such a determination, but were included in our results in alternate categories (as described in the following section, "Research Methodology").

Fourth, the study team was limited in its ability to interface with union personnel in the determination and assessment of evaluative findings. Such interaction would have required extensive prior coordination, authorizations, and multilevel reviews and approvals on behalf of the government and multiple union organizations (many government agencies interface and operate with a large number of different unions at a single location) that were beyond the scope of this study. Despite this restriction, we did make a number of union-related observations based on interviews with key civilian personnel leaders and our review of similar union issues encountered under the NSPS. These observations did not benefit from or incorporate the perspectives of union personnel or management.

Research Methodology

Our study results were informed by multiple data sources of program outcomes within the context of a comprehensive literature review. This section outlines the principal steps of our methodology and how these steps concluded in identification of effective practices and additional insights regarding management and oversight of program evaluations in the areas of workforce hiring, recruitment, and related compensation areas. The main steps of our methodology included a literature review and initial analysis, compiling a list of demonstration projects and APSs, structured interviews, and a structured approach to identifying effective practice types.

Literature Review and Initial Analysis

We conducted a literature review to understand the historical context of current and past demonstration projects, APSs, and direct-hire authorities within the scope of our study. Analysis of this review provided a baseline for identifying all organizational practices and determining which among them should be considered effective. An important part of this review was to gather information on the fundamental reasons why federal agencies initially implemented the desired practice flexibilities—information that informed the approach we later used to categorize the practices. This literature compilation documented those organizational areas of need and contributed to the cross-agency comparisons of practices.

Data analyses of publicly available survey sources—the FEVS and the Merit Principles Survey—supplemented this literature review. Such results provided an employee, supervisor, and management perspective—albeit a rather high-level one—on recruiting, hiring, and compensation practices. These quantitative and objective data offered one view of the possible impacts of organizational practices independent of perspectives gained during interviews with organization leadership.

Finally, we conducted interviews with civilian personnel representatives from the military departments and the intelligence and acquisition communities to gain broad perspectives of the policy justifications for past program requests and to ensure that we had a comprehensive and up-to-date listing of all programs (within the constraints noted previously).

Compiling a List of Demonstration Projects and Alternative Personnel Systems and Their Evaluations

In 2008, the OPM published its last review of the demonstration projects and APSs being used throughout the federal government. As a part of its efforts to document innovations pursued and results of these various systems, the OPM released four reports that described each of the then current demonstration projects and APSs and how they had changed over the prior year. (Appendix A describes each of these projects.) The first report, issued in 2005, summarized the first 25 years of experience with demonstration projects and APSs. Reports published in 2006, 2007, and 2008 covered different aspects of the demonstration projects and APSs.[14] Since the last report was published, in 2008, the OPM has not published any reviews or compilations of new or expanded demonstration projects or APSs.

This study will serve as the first documented compilation of demonstration projects and APSs since the OPM's 2008 report and serves as a reference point for discussing these systems and their evaluations. To compile a current list of systems and projects, we determined whether each of the systems in the 2008 report was still functioning as of May 2019 and whether new systems and projects had begun since that time. This was accomplished through internet searches and an examination of Federal Register Notices (FRNs) that some systems were required to submit when alterations were proposed. Most of the systems listed in the OPM's 2008 report are still in place; however, some have expired or been repealed.[15]

---

[14] OPM, 2007.

[15] DoD's NSPS was repealed with the signing of the 2010 Defense Authorization Act. The ATF's personnel management demonstration project was terminated in 28 U.S.C., Section

We then sought to validate the initial list of demonstration projects and APSs compiled by the study team. Accordingly, we interviewed multiple OPM representatives who were familiar with and responsible for past demonstration efforts. We also contacted select members of the Chief Human Capital Officers Council, the interagency forum responsible for corporately implementing and monitoring the PMA. To finalize our compilation and determine any remaining sources for past work regarding governmental effective practices for hiring, recruiting, and related compensation areas, we engaged multiple fellows from the National Academy of Public Administration (NAPA).

As a means to organize our follow-on analysis and to test for potential differences in program practices and outcomes, we grouped the demonstration projects and APSs into four broad categories:

1. OPM-approved demonstration projects authorized under 5 U.S.C., Chapter 47, that provide an exemption to certain parts of 5 U.S.C., the section of the U.S.C. that outlines federal HR laws.

2. agency-managed demonstration projects; these projects are still under certain provisions of 5 U.S.C., Chapter 47, but the agency involved has been authorized the oversight and approval authority.

3. APSs that were initially demonstration projects, have been made permanent, and now operate independently of the OPM and 5 U.S.C.

4. other independent personnel systems created outside the purview of 5 U.S.C. to meet the specific personnel management needs of various federal agencies.[16]

599B, in 2016. The Alcohol and Tobacco Tax and Trade Bureau's pay demonstration was discontinued in 2014 according to its fiscal year (FY) 2014 President's Budget. See Alcohol and Tobacco Tax and Trade Bureau, *FY 2014 President's Budget*, Washington, D.C.: Alcohol and Tobacco Tax and Trade Bureau, 2014, pp. TTB-14–TTB-15.

[16] The flexibilities discussed in this study are not limited by these categories of demonstration projects or APSs. For example, pay banding is found in all four categories of alternative systems.

We also supplemented our list of demonstration projects and APSs with a consideration of other direct-hire authorities (DHAs). DHAs are either government-wide or specific to a particular agency, and they may have been authorized through legislation or granted by the OPM. Although DHAs are not technically APSs, we included such programs to be comprehensive in our analysis and in recognition of the recent proliferation of this type of recruitment authority and its impact on hiring.

Using this comprehensive and finalized list, we collected detailed background and evaluative information of program purposes, initiating guidance, outcomes, impacts, and revisions made to the programs over time. We worked with all relevant organizations to collect available high-quality data—preferably objective evaluations published by external qualified sources. For example, the Department of Commerce's (DoC's) Commerce Alternative Personnel System (CAPS) annual evaluations are publicly available on the agency's website. Others were made available by the organization that conducted the evaluation, such as the 2016 Personnel Reform Effectiveness Assessment of the Federal Aviation Administration (FAA) and RAND's multiple assessments of the DoD Civilian Acquisition Workforce Demonstration Project (AcqDemo).

For those programs in which evaluations were not available, releasable, or deemed valid, we sought the highest-quality data available from alternative sources—primarily published FRNs and structured interviews with program subject matter experts.

Structured Interviews

Because the study team was unable to systematically use evaluations to identify effective practices for demonstration projects and APSs, the team conducted interviews with senior leaders, officials, and subject matter experts from various organizations and agencies that have or have had personnel demonstration projects or APSs.[17] The purpose of

---

[17] All RAND studies are screened for involvement of human subjects to ensure that human subjects protection requirements are observed. Following the requirements in Title 45 of the Code of Federal Regulations, Part 46, a study is reviewed, by RAND and potentially the

the interviews was to learn specifically about the successful practices of the various programs, documented program outcomes, and features of the systems that stood out as potential effective practices. The study team developed a protocol to gather factual information on the flexibilities that were granted outside of the general 5 U.S.C. system.[18] (The complete interview protocol is reproduced in Appendix C.)

To prepare for these interviews and inform development of the interview protocol, the study team drew on the review of relevant literature discussed earlier. This review included FRNs, legislation, and other literature regarding alternative hiring, recruiting, and compensation practices across the federal government; GAO reports; OPM documents on establishing and evaluating demonstration projects; articles; RAND reports; and other scholarly papers. The team also reviewed available evaluations of demonstration projects or APSs.

The interviews began with the study team asking for background and factual information, such as starting dates for the demonstration projects and APSs, permanency of the flexibilities, reasoning behind requesting authorities, and which flexibilities have been (or were) granted. Participants were asked about the impact of the authorities on their ability to locate and hire quality candidates. The interviewees were also asked about the success and effectiveness of their HR policies or process changes, and any lessons in the implementation and management of these changes that would be beneficial to others looking to make similar changes.

These questions were open-ended and allowed for any types of practice considerations (i.e., not just hiring and compensation) that should be made when looking outside 5 U.S.C. authorities. Several questions sought information about evaluations that have been conducted on the participants' demonstration projects or APSs, and interviewers requested a copy of the evaluations for review. Some interview-

---

DoD Component sponsoring the study, to determine if the study is exempt or covered under protections for research involving human subjects. The human subjects protection determination was that the present project was not research and not a human subjects research project.

[18] PMA, undated.

ees were able to share their evaluations, while others either did not have evaluations that could be released publicly or had not yet completed evaluations.

Participants were also asked for information about tracking the effectiveness of their recruitment and hiring efforts, as well as manager satisfaction with recruitment and hiring, to further identify efforts related to PMA Subgoal 3. Additionally, participants were asked to share other flexibilities that they felt were needed to improve hiring and recruiting, and which of these they would be requesting going forward. Interviewers also sought information about issues associated with union bargaining and if the union workforce was (or is) covered by the demonstration project or APS. Asking about points of conflict between the demonstration project or APS and other parts of the agency, either due to differing authorities or compensation levels, provided further insight on crucial considerations for those looking into non–5 U.S.C. authorities.

Identification of Effective Practice Types
Using the information derived from the literature review, evaluations, and interviews, we developed a list of practices that covered the initiatives employed in demonstration projects, APSs, and DHAs. This population of practices evolved and was refined based on our examination of the initiating legislative language and FRNs for the respective programs. We had HR professionals—both current and former government employees—review and validate this listing for completeness.

Because the resulting list of practices varied and was inconsistent in terms of specificity, we conducted a content analysis of all the practices, identified themes for consistent practice classifications, coded practices into these themes, compared practices both within and across themes, examined frequencies of themes to determine if categories should be collapsed or expanded, and conducted independent replication of the process. The net result was a consistent and common list of practice types associated with each personnel program. This work facilitated cross-agency comparisons of practices and their eventual classification into one of three categories of effectiveness: best, promising, and innovative.

While the PMA characterizes high-level practices under the rubric of "best practices," we examined the broader concept of effective practices, for which best practices is a subset. We applied the following definitions and standards for determining and categorizing various types of noted organizational practices:

- **Effective practices:** Systematic examination of an organization's activities, strategies, methods, systems, processes, techniques, tactics, and approaches that have defined parameters that can be assessed and compared with similar practices to generate successful outcomes or have a positive impact.
- **Best practices:** Practices that have been proven to help organizations reach high levels of efficiency or effectiveness and produce successful outcomes. Best practices are evidence based and proven effective through objective and comprehensive research and evaluation.
- **Promising practices:** Practices that have been shown to work effectively and produce successful outcomes. Promising practices are supported, to some degree, by objective data (e.g., feedback from subject matter experts, results of external audits) and subjective data (e.g., interviews, anecdotal reports of practice implementers) but are not validated through the same rigorous approach as best practices.
- **Innovative practices:** Practices that have worked within one organization and show promise during its early stages for progressing to more demonstrated impact. Innovative practices have some objective basis for claiming effectiveness and potential for replication to other organizations.[19]

Based on these broad definitions, Table 1.1 provides further details into a range of criteria that describe the data, information, and characteristics that led to the specification of the three effective practice types.

---

[19] Definitions and standards for the concept of effective practices are adapted from Compassion Capital Fund National Resource Center, *Identifying and Promoting Effective Practices*, Washington, D.C.: Compassion Capital Fund National Resource Center, undated, p. 5.

Table 1.1
Criteria Characterizing Types of Effective Practices

Best practice	• Proven effectiveness in addressing a common problem • Proven effectiveness in more than one organization and in more than one context • Replication on a broad scale • Conclusive data from comparison to objective benchmarks, with positive results • Conclusive data from a comprehensive objective evaluation by an external, qualified source
Promising practice	• Effectiveness in addressing a common problem • Effectiveness in more than one organization and in more than one context • Replication on a limited scale • Supporting data from comparison to objective benchmarks, with positive results • Supporting data from an internal assessment or external evaluation
Innovative practice	• Suggested effectiveness in addressing a common problem • Successful use in one organization and context • Potential for replication • Limited supporting data from comparison to objective benchmarks, with positive results • Limited supporting data from internal assessment

SOURCE: Adapted from Compassion Capital Fund National Resource Center, undated, p. 5.

While such data specifications and criteria may appear straightforward and definitive, there is interpretation involved as to how each factor is accurately defined and to what extent data are available and valid in addressing these criteria. Even if data are readily available, judgment is required in determining respective thresholds to assess if the practice definition has been sufficiently satisfied.

We used the criteria in Table 1.1 to examine the full list of common practice types to determine which could be classified as "effective" and then to establish the appropriate variant of effectiveness—best, promising, or innovative. We applied the effectiveness criteria to each practice, using them as reasonable guidelines rather than strict and inflexible thresholds. To counter the potential for inconsistent application of these standards, multiple HR professionals on the research team who have considerable operational experience independently made effectiveness and categorization judgments of practice types. After these initial assessments, the group convened to compare results and discuss its decision logic. A second round of independent judging allowed the professionals to reassess their classifications. The outcome was consistent agreement in the determination and categorization of effective practice types.

We examined the results of best, promising, and innovative practice types within the three personnel areas of hiring, recruiting, and related compensation areas and considered implications for implementation at DoD. Despite the absence of a standardized process for evaluating personnel reform, we highlight in this report effective practices for DoD's consideration as a starting point for future and more data-driven analysis.

Considerations for Improving Assessment and Dissemination of Effective Practices

Our systematic review of program practices resulted in a secondary outcome of interest to the project sponsor, who requested its inclusion in this report: issues associated with specification, conduct, oversight, and reporting of evaluation *processes* for demonstration projects and APSs. Federal responsibility for these roles has changed over time. In some areas this has resulted in ambiguity in requirements and voids in accountability. Through our extensive interactions with DoD and federal agencies, we identified a range of issues associated with these processes. Because we did not systematically research and analyze such issues, we do not offer specific recommendations for how these issues should be resolved but instead offer observations and considerations that DoD and other federal agencies may explore or develop further.

The Structure of This Report

Chapter Two discusses the findings of the literature review and survey analysis. It describes the motivation that led various federal agencies to seek and adopt recruiting, hiring, and relevant compensation flexibilities and the major changes in the way these flexibilities have been implemented over time. Chapter Three provides information on the history of demonstration projects and APSs and focuses on those that were active from 2008 to May 2019. Chapter Four examines effective practices from the APSs, demonstration projects and DHAs related to recruiting and hiring, and highlights any data collection or analytical efforts that examined the outcomes of these reforms. As mentioned previously, DHAs are not technically APSs but were have been to the review because of the recent proliferation of this type of recruitment authority and its impact on hiring. Chapter Five provides observations and considerations to help the OPM better leverage HR management reform efforts and track their outcomes, with an eye toward improving HR management across the federal government. Conclusions can be found in Chapter Six.

CHAPTER TWO

A Brief Historical Overview of Demonstration Projects, Alternative Personnel Systems, and Direct-Hire Authorities

The purpose of the chapter is to provide some historical context behind the development of various APSs in the federal government in recent decades based on our literature review. It starts with a description of the circumstances that led to the enactment of the 1978 CSRA and the birth of OPM-approved personnel demonstration projects and APSs that developed as a result of the new personnel management flexibilities the CSRA provided. The chapter then discusses the policy conditions that spurred the establishment of additional independent APSs, codified in law and tailored to meet the individual needs of specific federal agencies. While the chapter provides a broad overview of the evolution of these various demonstration projects and APSs, a description of the systems can be found in Appendix A. Additional information on DHAs, which provide additional flexibilities in an agency's ability to hire the right talent but also increase the complexity of federal HR systems, is given in Appendix B.

The Civil Service Reform Act and the Original Demonstration Projects

In 1978, the administration of President Jimmy Carter saw an opportunity to reform the system, enacting a series of reforms in the CSRA related to pay-for-performance practices and improving the recruitment and retention of talent. Before the CSRA, more than 6,000 pages of civil service laws, procedures, and regulations governed the federal human capital system.[1] That system—established under the Pendleton Civil Service Reform Act in 1883—developed gradually over the years, driven by prevailing political winds in the White House and Congress and a 1920s turn toward scientific management principles that emphasized the need for standard duty classifications and compensation levels.[2] The accretion of policies and procedures over time led to a complex, uneven system that struggled to balance the tension between avoiding a spoils system based on political favor and adopting an overly rigid system that failed to recognize and reward employees based on merit. The most significant of these reforms are

- the establishment of the OPM, replacing the Civil Service Commission, which was abolished
- the establishment of the Merit Systems Protection Board, which codified merit-based principles
- the establishment of the Federal Labor Relations Authority, which described prohibited personnel practices
- the creation of the Senior Executive Service, which established a corps of executive leadership above GS-15 in the General Schedule (GS) system.[3]

These reforms were incorporated into 5 U.S.C., which includes the statutes governing the management of administrative personnel in federal agencies.

In many ways, however, the CSRA marked only the beginning of 5 U.S.C. reform. Most relevant to this report, the CSRA did not

---

[1]   "The History of Civil Service Reform," in George T. Milkovich and Alexandra K. Wigdor, eds., *Pay for Performance: Evaluating Performance Appraisal and Merit Pay*, Washington, D.C.: National Academies Press, 1991, p. 17.

[2]   "The History of Civil Service Reform," 1991, pp. 13–17.

[3]   Margaret Weichert, "OPM Celebrates 40th Anniversary of Civil Service Reform Act," *Our Director: U.S. Office of Personnel Management Director's Blog*, October 12, 2018.

provide for the comprehensive reform of basic hiring procedures.[4] Recognizing that special interests might resist change in many areas, the presidential commission established to make recommendations to inform the CSRA—known as the President's Personnel Management Project—took a cautious approach that often favored experimentation over permanent, comprehensive change.[5]

In the case of hiring procedures, this meant leaning heavily on demonstration projects to strengthen the case for reform. The CSRA created 5 U.S.C., Chapter 47, Personnel, Research Programs and Demonstration Projects, which authorized the newly created OPM to establish and maintain (and assist in the establishment and maintenance of) research programs to study improved methods and technologies in federal personnel management. While the law did not limit these demonstration projects to recruiting and hiring, federal agencies have leveraged the flexibility to make significant changes in the way they conduct these activities.

The CSRA created the opportunity for federal agencies to try innovations in federal HR management by developing demonstration projects that could waive various sections of 5 U.S.C. related to

- methods of establishing qualification requirements for, recruitment for, and appointment to positions
- methods of classifying positions and compensating employees
- methods of assigning, reassigning, or promoting employees
- methods of disciplining employees
- methods of providing incentives to employees, including the provision of group or individual incentive bonuses or pay
- hours of work per day or per week
- methods of involving employees, labor organizations, and employee organizations in personnel decisions
- methods of reducing overall agency staff and grade levels.[6]

---

[4] "The History of Civil Service Reform," 1991, p. 17.

[5] Carolyn Ban, "QED: The Research and Demonstration Provisions of the Civil Service Reform Act," *Policy Studies Journal*, Vol. 17, No. 2, Winter 1988–1989, p. 420.

[6] U.S.C., Title 5, Section 4703, Demonstration Projects, August 13, 2018.

Each project could involve a maximum of 5,000 employees. Title 5 of the U.S.C., Chapter 47, mandates that the demonstration projects should not last more than five years, but it also granted a generous exception, stating that projects could continue beyond that date "to the extent necessary to validate results of the project."[7] Beginning in 1980 and continuing today, a number of demonstration projects have been authorized under 5 U.S.C., Chapter 47, though only a total of ten demonstration projects can be ongoing at one time. Table 2.1 provides a list of demonstration projects authorized by the OPM or that required OPM approval.[8]

The first demonstration project was the U.S. Navy Demonstration Project, also known as China Lake. Established in 1980, it included both the Naval Weapons Center in China Lake, California, and the Naval Ocean Systems Center in San Diego. The underlying purpose of the project was to expand managerial control over personnel functions, create a more responsible personnel system, and create an integrated approach to pay, performance, and classification.[9] To accomplish these goals, China Lake implemented several innovations to its personnel system.

The most notable reform concerned the concept of pay banding, which allowed employees to be paid outside of the traditional 5 U.S.C. GS system. Instead of positions being classified within one of the 15 GS grades, China Lake grouped positions into five pay bands based on the type of work performed. In this new system, multiple grades were combined into a pay band, which allowed for a greater range of duties to be performed and salary paid for any one position. Employees in this system could be paid more or less than in the traditional system, and

---

[7]   U.S.C, Title 5, Section 4703.

[8]   The OPM puts the number at 18, but the now-expired Federal Bureau of Investigation demonstration project was not authorized under the CSRA; rather, the FY 1988 Intelligence Authorization Act required that the OPM and the Federal Bureau of Investigation jointly conduct the demonstration. See OPM, 2007, p. 8, n. 3.

[9]   45 Fed. Reg. 26504, U.S. Office of Personnel Management, Proposed Demonstration Project: An Integrated Approach to Pay, Performance Appraisal, and Position Classification for More Effective Operation of Government Organizations, April 18, 1980.

Table 2.1
Office of Personnel Management–Approved Personnel Demonstration
Projects Authorized Under Title 5 of the U.S. Code

Demonstration Projects	Innovations Sought	Year Initiated	Status
DoD Navy Demonstration Project (China Lake)	• Pay banding • Pay for performance • Higher starting salary • Recruitment bonuses	1980	Now an APS
Department of Transportation (DoT) FAA Airway Science Curriculum (FAA I)	• Alternative selection process	1982	Expired in 1993
Air Force PACER SHARE	• Pay banding • Group performance rating • Gainsharing • Relocation bonuses	1988	Expired in 1993
DoC National Institute of Standards and Technology (NIST)	• Pay bonding • Pay for performance • Expedited hiring • Recruitment and retention bonuses	1988	Extended Indefinitely
DoT FAA Demonstration Project (FAA II)	• Retention bonuses	1989	Expired in 1994
U.S. Department of Agriculture (USDA)	• Category rating • DHA • Recruitment incentives	1990	Now an APS
DoC	• Pay banding • Pay for performance	1998	Now an APS
DoD Acquisition Workforce	• Pay banding • Pay for performance • Streamlining hiring	1998	Transitioned to DoD authority in 2017

Table 2.1—Continued

Demonstration Projects	Innovations Sought	Year Initiated	Status
DoD Science and Technology Labs[a]	• Pay banding • Pay for performance • DHA	1997	Transitioned to DoD authority in 2000
Air Force Research Laboratory (AFRL)		1997	
Army Aviation and Missile Research, Development and Engineering Center		1997	
Army Research Laboratory		1998	
Army Medical Research and Materiel Command		1998	
Naval Sea Systems Command (NAVSEA) Surface Warfare Center		1998	
Army Engineering Research and Development Center		1998	
Naval Research Laboratory		1999	
Department of Energy (DoE)/National Nuclear Security Administration (NNSA)	• Pay banding • Pay for performance • Improved hiring • Simplified position and description • Motivation and retention of staff	2006	Transitioned to DoE authority in 2008

SOURCE: Data collected from James R. Thompson, "Personnel Demonstration Projects and Human Resource Management Innovation," *Review of Public Personnel Administration*, Vol. 28, No. 3, 2008, pp. 240–262, and from OPM, 2007, p. 8, n. 3.

[a] This list does not include demonstration projects managed by DoD after the department received demonstration authority in 2001. This includes lab demonstrations established after the Laboratory Demonstration Project (Lab Demo) was transitioned to DoD in 2001.

supervisors were able to have more control over the work they asked the employee to perform and the compensation paid.

Supervisors were also expected to develop performance plans with the goal of effectively communicating employees' responsibilities and supervisors' expectations. Additionally, supervisors were instructed to conduct two progress reviews at the fifth and ninth months of the performance cycle. Employees were encouraged to list their accomplishments for these progress reviews. China Lake also permitted reduction-in-force procedures that aimed to increase retention of the most capable employees. This involved ranking the employees first by their performance and then retention standings.

The practice of pay banding proved successful in the China Lake demonstration project. As a result, in 1995 Congress repealed its temporary status as a demonstration project and identified it as the first permanent APS that evolved from the 5 U.S.C., Chapter 47, demonstration projects.[10] Other demonstration projects followed suit; projects at the DoC and the USDA were converted to APSs in 1998. After the OPM rejected a request from NIST to establish a demonstration project mirroring China Lake on the grounds that it was too similar, Congress approved NIST's request to become a personnel demonstration project in 1987.[11] In March 1996, the NIST demonstration project was extended indefinitely.[12]

Other federal agencies also drew on China Lake's pioneering use of pay banding. By 2008, at least nine federal agencies and almost 300,000 federal employees were covered by pay banding.[13] This means that 15 percent of federal employees were in HR systems that used pay banding demonstrating the continuing trend of agencies wanting to use this HR toll and its inherent flexibilities. In addition, China Lake's

---

[10] Public Law 103-337, National Defense Authorization Act for Fiscal Year 1995, October 5, 1994.

[11] Thompson, 2008, p. 243.

[12] Public Law 104-113, National Technology Transfer and Advancement Act of 1995, Section 10, Personnel, March 7, 1996.

[13] Thompson, 2008, p. 245.

effective use of retention bonuses to retain personnel who might otherwise leave for jobs outside the department prompted the inclusion of such bonuses in the Federal Employees Pay Comparability Act of 1990. In addition to other changes in federal pay administration, the act included authorities that authorized other federal agencies to use various bonuses and other flexibilities leveraged by other demonstration projects within FAA II, NIST, and the USDA, among others.

Competing for Highly Skilled Workers

Two emerging trends in Western economies have changed the hiring landscape, making it more challenging for DoD to compete with the private sector for highly skilled workers. The first trend is the emergence of the so-called knowledge economy, which places greater emphasis on intellectual assets (or knowledge) than physical assets.[14] In this context, federal workers will increasingly need deep, highly specialized knowledge to provide knowledge services and adapt to technological innovations. Second, changes in information technology were beginning to upend long-held assumptions about the tools workers would use to do their jobs and dramatically reduced the need for clerical workers. Senior managers were starting to use their own phones, schedule their own meetings, and, eventually, would send their own emails.[15] These changes required personnel management reforms designed to modernize the GS classification and pay system, built largely around a rigid compensation system designed for a 1940s-era clerical workforce.

To remain competitive in this dynamic environment, DoD requested and received authority in the FY 1995 National Defense Authorization Act (NDAA) to conduct personnel demonstrations under OPM authority for various DoD STRLs. These demonstrations would

---

[14] Walter W. Powell and Kaisa Snellman, "The Knowledge Economy," *Annual Review of Sociology*, Vol. 30, August 11, 2004, pp. 199–220.

[15] Lisa Rein, "As Federal Government Evolves, Its Clerical Workers Edge Toward Extinction," *Washington Post*, January 14, 2014.

come to be known as Lab Demo.[16] In addition, in the FY 1996 NDAA, DoD received authority to establish yet another OPM-approved demonstration project, known as AcqDemo.[17] Both AcqDemo—which allowed DoD to develop HR management systems for its scientist and engineering and acquisition workforces, respectively, outside of 5 U.S.C.—and Lab Demo used China Lake's pay banding concept and paired it with a streamlined job classification system; it was the first time a deviation occurred from the established OPM classification system and allowed employees in newly streamlined position categories to perform a broader range of work and receive a broader range of pay. The practice of pay banding, which continues today, reflected the growing emphasis on the recruitment and retention of workers with specific skills and experience rather than the recruitment of workers to perform a discrete set of tasks for a narrowly defined position.

AcqDemo was temporarily subsumed in the now-canceled NSPS, discussed further below, but became a demonstration project outside the purview of the OPM upon the dissolution of the NSPS in 2011.[18]

The Growth of Independent Systems Outside the Office of Personnel Management's Purview

Despite the widespread interest in mirroring the perceived success of China Lake, OPM-approved demonstration projects were relatively few in number for at least three reasons. First, according to the GAO, federal agencies perceived that the OPM was not interested in supporting demonstration projects; throughout the 1980s, the agency did not

---

[16] Public Law 103-337, National Defense Authorization Act for Fiscal Year 1995, Title III, Subtitle E, Civilian Employees, Section 342(b), Defense Laboratories Personnel Demonstration Projects, October 5, 1994.

[17] Jennifer Lamping Lewis et al., *2016 Assessment of the Civilian Acquisition Workforce Personnel Demonstration Project*, Santa Monica, Calif.: RAND Corporation, RR-1783-OSD, 2016, p. 1.

[18] 82 Fed. Reg. 52104, Department of Defense, Acquisition Workforce Personnel Demonstration (AcqDemo) Project, November 9, 2017.

take a proactive role in encouraging federal agencies to establish dem-onstration projects and track their outcomes.[19] Second, in keeping with the spirit of the demonstration projects as set forth in 5 U.S.C. and expanded on by the OPM in regulations in 5 C.F.R., the number of demonstration projects was purposefully limited on the grounds that they were opportunities for experimentation, which might eventually lead to government-wide reforms, as opposed to permanent fixes for the specific personnel management problems of various government agen-cies.[20] Third, federal agencies faced a variety of statutory and financial hurdles to establishing formal OPM-approved demonstration projects. Statutory constraints include requirements to hold public hearings, a limitation of ten demonstration projects at any one time, a limitation on the number of employees in a demonstration project to 5,000, and a requirement for federal agencies to seek legislative approval to convert their demonstration projects into permanent APSs.[21]

In light of these hurdles, some federal agencies began to pursue legislative relief to establish their own independent systems outside the purview of the OPM. For example, the Financial Institutions Reform, Recovery and Enforcement Act of 1989 (FIRREA) granted federal financial regulatory agencies—including the Farm Credit Adminis-tration, the National Credit Union Administration (NCUA), and the Office of the Comptroller of the Currency (OCC), among others who would join later—the flexibility to establish their own personnel sys-tems.[22] The FAA also established an independent system in 1996 based on the FAA's HR system under 49 U.S.C., Section 40122.

However, it was after the September 11, 2001, attacks that federal agencies' level of interest in independent personnel systems increased most notably.

---

[19] GAO, *Federal Personnel: Status of Personnel Research and Demonstration Projects*, Wash-ington, D.C.: U.S. Government Accountability Office, GGD-87-116BR, September 1987.

[20] Thompson, 2008, p. 245.

[21] Beth S. Slavet et al., *The U.S. Office of Personnel Management in Retrospect: Achievements and Challenges After Two Decades*, Washington, D.C.: U.S. Merit Systems Protection Board Office of Policy and Evaluation, December 2001, p. 40.

[22] OPM, 2007, p. 25.

In the early 2000s, Congress established the next wave of APSs under separate authorities unrelated to personnel demonstration projects. Labor union resistance to these additional legislative reforms, based on a concern that pay banding would give too much discretion to managers, was mitigated by strong support for these reforms in the Republican-controlled Congress and White House.[23] In line with this sentiment, the 2002 PMA supported managerial flexibility and the tailoring of personnel systems to agency needs.[24] Presidential and congressional support for personnel management flexibilities was further reinvigorated in the wake of the September 11, 2001, attacks, with the administration of President George W. Bush and some lawmakers increasingly viewing perceived inefficiencies in personnel management as a national security risk.[25]

In 2002 Congress enacted legislation establishing the Department of Homeland Security (DHS) that included a provision authorizing the establishment of the department's own personnel system,[26] known as MaxHR, which included rules governing performance management, labor relations, adverse actions, and appeals. It also featured a market- and performance-based pay approach to replace the decades-old GS system. But a series of court rulings in 2006 prohibited DHS from moving forward with its modified approach to labor relations deviating from 5 U.S.C. requirements, and in early 2007 DHS decided to hold off on implementing a pay-for-performance system.

The department also announced a broader initiative—the Human Capital Operational Plan—to promote hiring and retention, learning and development, and a DHS-wide integrated leadership system. A provision in the FY 2009 Consolidated Security, Disaster Assistance and Continuing Appropriations Act, Public Law 110-329, prohibited spending funds to operate the new DHS HR management

---

[23] Thompson, 2008, pp. 252–253.

[24] OPM, *The President's Management Agenda*, Washington, D.C.: U.S. Office of Management and Budget, 2002.

[25] Thompson, 2008, p. 259.

[26] Public Law 107-296, Homeland Security Act of 2002, November 25, 2002.

system and repealed rules governing labor relations and adverse actions and appeals—returning DHS employees to 5 U.S.C. coverage. The law also eliminated pay for performance at DHS, except at the Transportation Security Administration (TSA), whose personnel system was established under a different statute, the Aviation and Transportation Security Act, Public Law 107-71, Section 114.

In 2003 DoD sent a proposal to Congress calling for new personnel management flexibilities, such as the authority to eliminate pay grades and steps in the legacy GS system in favor of pay banding.[27] The flexibilities were successfully codified in the FY 2004 NDAA, setting the stage for DoD to establish the NSPS, a sweeping reform effort providing DoD a new HR management system that included, among other things, a pay band system to replace the GS grade and step system, simplify hiring, extended probationary periods, new compensation practices, and a new performance management system that included pay for performance. While it was intended for the entire department, excluding only Lab Demo projects, it covered 211,000 DoD employees under its phased implementation.[28] The NSPS proved to be controversial and was the subject of legal challenges through the federal court system. On November 7, 2005, a coalition of ten unions that represented DoD employees filed a lawsuit in federal district court challenging the DoD's final regulations for the NSPS published in the Federal Register. The union's case to halt implementation of the NSPS went all the way to the U.S. Supreme Court. On September 5, 2007, the Court denied the motion for a stay, and DoD continued its implementation of the NSPS.[29]

In 2011 the NSPS was repealed following years of vocal opposition from federal employee unions that argued that it was unfair because it violated a worker's right to collectively bargain and that the merit-

---

[27] Wendy R. Ginsberg, *Pay-for-Performance: Lessons from the National Security Personnel System*, Washington, D.C.: Congressional Research Service, RL34673, December 18, 2009, p. 3.

[28] Ginsberg, 2009, p. 3.

[29] Ginsberg, 2009, p. 20.

based pay system was subjective and implemented inconsistently.[30] In a campaign promise letter to the International Federation of Professional and Technical Engineers, Senator Barack Obama expressed his support for reversing the NSPS.[31] President Barack Obama followed through with his campaign promise and signed into law a bill abolishing the NSPS on October 28, 2009.[32]

---

[30] Ginsberg, 2009, pp.14–18.

[31] Federal Soup, "NSPS—National Security Personnel System," webpage, undated.

[32] Public Law 111-84, National Defense Authorization Act for Fiscal Year 2010, October 28, 2009.

CHAPTER THREE

Current Demonstration Projects and Alternative Personnel Systems

As was explained in Chapter One, the study team identified four categories of demonstration projects and APSs:

- OPM-approved demonstration projects
- agency-managed demonstration projects
- APSs that were former demonstration projects
- other independent personnel systems outside the purview of 5 U.S.C.

In this chapter we discuss the current demonstration projects and APSs that are operating in the federal government. Table 3.1 provides a summary of these current projects and systems, as well as a range of other information regarding the availability of evaluations, whether supplemental interviews were conducted, and the flexibilities desired by the implemented practice. We begin first by describing the requirements for the OPM demonstration projects before discussing the different demonstration projects and APS that exist. The chapter closes with a consolidated look at all the different demonstration projects and APSs currently in operation along with identification of available project evaluations.

Table 3.1
Synopsis of Current Federal Human Resources Demonstrations and Alternative Personnel Systems

Name	Date Authorized	Publicly Available Evaluation	Supplemental Interview	Practice Themes
Agency-Managed Demonstration Projects				
DoD, AcqDemo	1999	Yes	Yes	Contribution-based compensation DHA Recruiting flexibilities Extended probationary period Market-based pay Pay banding Advanced in-hire rates Pay review and leveling
DoD, Lab Demo	1997	Cited but not available	Yes	Pay banding Pay for performance DHA Extended probationary period Recruiting flexibilities Contribution-based compensation Advanced in-hire rates Scholastic achievement appointments
DoE, NNSA	2006	Yes	Yes	Pay banding Pay for performance Improved hiring Simplified position description

Table 3.1—Continued

Name	Date Authorized	Publicly Available Evaluation	Supplemental Interview	Practice Themes
APSs That Were Former Demonstration Projects				
China Lake	1986	Yes	Yes	Pay banding Pay for performance Higher starting salary Recruitment bonuses
DoC, NIST	1986	Cited but not available	Yes	Pay banding Pay for performance Expedited hiring Recruitment and retention bonuses Recruiting flexibilities DHA Advanced in-hire rates
DoC, CAPS	1998	Yes	No	Pay banding Pay for performance Expedited hiring Recruitment and retention bonuses Extended probationary period Advanced in-hire rates Contribution-based compensation
USDA, Agriculture Research Service (ARS)	1981	Yes	Yes	Category rating DHA Recruitment incentives Extended probationary period

Table 3.1—Continued

Name	Date Authorized	Publicly Available Evaluation	Supplemental Interview	Practice Themes
Independent Personnel Systems Outside 5 U.S.C.				
DOT, FAA	1996	Yes	Yes	Alternative selection process Retention bonuses Pay banding Recruiting flexibilities DHA
Department of the Treasury, Internal Revenue Service (IRS)	1998	Yes	No	Pay banding Pay for performance
GAO	1980	Yes	No	Pay banding Pay for performance Early retirement options Competitive pay rates Market-based pay
DHS, TSA	2001	Yes	Yes	Pay for performance Recruiting flexibilities
Defense Civilian Intelligence Personnel System (DCIPS)	1996	Cited but not available	Yes	Pay banding Recruiting flexibilities DHA Pay review and leveling
DoD, Cyber Excepted Service (CES)	2016	No	Yes	Recruiting flexibilities Market-based pay Advanced in-hire rates DHA
DHS, CES (Cybersecurity Workforce)	2016	No	Yes	Recruiting flexibilities

Table 3.1—Continued

Name	Date Authorized	Publicly Available Evaluation	Supplemental Interview	Practice Themes
Department of Veterans Affairs (VA)	1983	No	Yes	Pay banding Recruiting flexibilities Pay for performance Market-based pay DHA
Other Independent Personnel Systems Outside the Purview of 5 U.S.C.				
Commodity Futures Trading Commission	2006	No	No	Pay banding Pay comparability Performance-based pay
Consumer Financial Protection Bureau	2011 (CFPB)	No	No	Pay banding Pay comparability Performance-based pay
Farm Credit Administration	1993	No	No	Pay banding Pay comparability Performance-based pay
Federal Deposit Insurance Corporation	2003	No	No	Pay banding Pay comparability Performance-based pay
Federal Housing Finance Agency	2008	No	No	Pay banding Pay comparability Performance-based pay
National Credit Union Administration (NCUA)	1992	No	Yes	Pay banding Pay comparability Performance-based pay Enhanced retirement and health benefits
Department of Treasury, OCC	1991	No	Yes	Pay banding Pay comparability Performance-based pay

Table 3.1—Continued

Name	Date Authorized	Publicly Available Evaluation	Supplemental Interview	Practice Themes
Department of Treasury, Office of Financial Research	2001	No	No	Pay banding Pay comparability Performance-based pay
Securities and Exchange Commission	2002	No	No	Pay banding Pay comparability Performance-based pay Recruitment incentives

Office of Personnel Management–Approved Demonstration Projects

An agency can obtain the authority to waive existing 5 U.S.C. provisions in order to propose and test interventions for its own personnel management system through an OPM-approved demonstration project. There are two ways such a project can be established: the first is through an agency requesting OPM approval of the project, and the second is through legislation that directs the head of an agency to develop and implement the project under 5 U.S.C., Chapter 47. The OPM issued the *Demonstration Projects Handbook*, which outlines the steps involved in development and approval of a demonstration project, and it encourages agencies to contact the office first before developing a formal request. The OPM would like agencies to be able to address the following questions:

- What specific organizational problems or needs will be addressed?
- How will the resolution of this problem or need help in accomplishing the organization's mission?
- What barriers prevent the agency from resolving this problem, and how will the demonstration project be used to remove these barriers?

- Is the action required to resolve the problem within the scope of the demonstration project authority?
- Does it require a waiver of 5 U.S.C. laws or regulations?
- What will be considered a success in terms of the purpose and objective of this demonstration project?[1]

The *Handbook* also outlines the steps involved in achieving approval for a demonstration project:

- **Developing a project plan.** Develop a plan with sufficient detail that it can be published in the Federal Register explaining all elements of the plan including those parts of 5 U.S.C. that will be waived.
- **Communicating the project plan.** Explain the plan, goals, and objectives to the employees who will be covered.
- **Approving and clearing the project plan.** Both agency approvals and OPM approvals are required.
- **Statutory notification requirements.** OPM will arrange for two Federal Register notices: one announcing the planned demonstration project, and a final notice that includes all responses to the first Federal Register notice and responses to those responses.[2]

Ninety days after the publication of the second Federal Register notice, the agency may implement the demonstration project. For those agencies with bargaining unit employees that might be covered, local bargaining must be accomplished before those employees can be covered by the flexibilities proposed under the demonstration project. If management and labor cannot reach an agreement, then bargaining unit employees may not be moved under the demonstration project.

There are no OPM-approved demonstration projects at this time. A number of demonstration projects that began under OPM approval

---

[1] OPM, *Demonstration Projects Handbook*, Washington, D.C.: U.S. Office of Personnel Management, nda.

[2] OPM, ndb.

have since been moved under the authority of various agencies. Those projects are discussed below.

Agency-Managed Demonstration Projects

Agencies can receive statutory authority to develop and operate demonstration projects as envisioned under 5 U.S.C., Chapter 47, that do not require OPM approval. DoD and DoE currently have authority to independently manage demonstration projects that began under OPM approval.

The DoE NNSA was initially established under the authority of 5 U.S.C., Chapter 47, as an OPM-approved demonstration project in 2006. In the FY 2018 NDAA, authority was provided for DoE to assume full authority over the demonstration project and to extend the demonstration project for ten years. This demonstration project can be expanded to cover personnel assigned to the Navy nuclear program. An evaluation was available for the NNSA demonstration project.

The AcqDemo and Lab Demo projects were initially established under 5 U.S.C., Chapter 47, demonstration project authority and were implemented by DoD with the approval of the OPM. When Section 1114 of the FY 2001 NDAA placed these demonstrations under the Secretary of Defense, they no longer counted toward the OPM's allotted ten demonstration projects. The AcqDemo is a highly evaluated system, and there was a DoD evaluation of eight of the Lab Demo projects in 2012.[3] There are 18 separate Lab Demo projects, each with the potential for different HR flexibilities, which collectively include

- DHA
- simplified delegated job classification
- pay banding
- contribution-based compensation
- performance-based pay

---

[3]   William Todd Cole, *Evaluation of the Legacy Science and Technology Reinvention Laboratories*, Washington, D.C.: Defense Civilian Personnel Advisory Service, 2012.

- the Voluntary Emeritus Corps
- the Expanded Developmental Opportunities Program
- the lab commander award authority
- the Delegated Recruitment, Relocation, and Retention Incentive Authority
- an extended probationary period
- pay-setting authority delegated to management
- relocation bonuses for students
- accelerated compensation for interns
- supervisory differential
- critical skills training
- education-based pay adjustment.[4]

Appendix A provides a detailed description and further information for the laboratory demonstration projects that are outlined in Table 3.1.

Alternative Personnel Systems: Former Demonstration Projects

Title 5 of the U.S.C., Chapter 47, contains a provision that allows demonstration projects to become permanent. If the flexibilities tested and changes established by the demonstration projects are deemed successful and sustainable, these changes may be made permanent through independent legislation. Currently there are four federal agencies with permanent APSs that were former demonstration projects under OPM approval authority: CAPS; the Navy Ocean Systems Center, San Diego, and the Naval Weapons Center, China Lake, California (both known as China Lake); NIST, and the USDA's ARS. Each of these systems is managed by the agency; they do not count against the OPM's limit of ten concurrently operating demonstration projects. Of the four systems, only NIST did not have a readily available evaluation.

---

[4] Michelle Williams, Laboratory Quality Enhancement Program Personnel Subpanel Chair, STRL Update Briefing, May 13, 2016.

Other Independent Personnel Systems Outside the Purview of Title 5 of the U.S. Code

Some agencies have been granted independent legislative authority to implement their own personnel systems. While these systems are run by the agencies with the authority, the OPM provides oversight and notifies the agencies when it foresees problems with implementing the system.[5] Seventeen of these systems were found across various government agencies. These systems included DCIPS for the DoD intelligence community (IC); the Department of the Treasury's IRS; DHS's CES and TSA; DoD's CES; DoT's FAA; the GAO; and the VA. Evaluations were found for the FAA, IC, and IRS, while documentation for the GAO and TSA reports were only mentioned and not publicly available. No evaluation was available for the VA. The DoD and DHS cybersecurity workforces are relatively new programs and have either just begun implementation or had not yet launched at the time of our research, so there are no evaluations available.

The financial regulatory agencies have the authority to create their own personnel and compensation systems. These systems all tie compensation to performance and the employees' contribution to the mission of the agency.[6] The nine agencies that have this authority are the CFPB; the Commodity Futures Trading Commission; the Department of the Treasury, OCC; the Farm Credit Administration; the Federal Deposit Insurance Corporation; the Federal Housing Finance Agency; the NCUA; the Office of Financial Research; and the Securities and Exchange Commission. Of these agencies, only the Securities and Exchange Commission had a publicly available evaluation; and the CFPB, Farm Credit Administration, and Federal Deposit Insurance Corporation had records of an evaluation. No evaluations were found for the Commodity Futures Trading Commission, the Federal Housing Finance Agency, the NCUA, the OCC, or the Office of Financial Research.

---

[5]   OPM, 2007, p. 2.

[6]   OPM, 2007, p. 20.

A Summary of Current Alternative Personnel Systems and Demonstrations

Table 3.1 highlights the demonstration projects and APSs that are functioning as of May 2019 and the availability of program evaluations. As the table shows, only eight program evaluations were available from which to draw effective practices. Thus, our understanding of effective practices drew substantially on information gathered during interviews with agency personnel and HR managers—the results of which are discussed in Chapter Four.

Examining Effective Practices for Recruitment, Hiring, and Related Aspects of Compensation

The initial charter for this study was to identify best practices for recruiting, hiring, and related aspects of compensation derived from the current demonstration projects and APSs. As discussed in Chapter One, we refined this task, in conjunction with the project sponsor, to consider effective practices that can be categorized into one of three categories: best, promising, or innovative practices. Based on the assembled data detailed in Chapter Three, this chapter applies our effective practice methodology to the population of practices implemented across agencies, and reports those results.

The effective practice results along with associated data on the outcomes of these reforms are organized into four sections: recruiting, hiring, related aspects of compensation reform, and crosscutting effective practices. These effective practices provide an excellent starting point for broader DoD and other government agency consideration, as well as future analyses that are more data driven. Chapter Five addresses observations and considerations for ways in which government agencies can better conduct program evaluations and more systematically collect necessary supporting evidence of program outcomes to support future analyses.

Recruiting

Effective practices used in recruiting are listed in Table 4.1. The table identifies the practice category and lists all agencies that the study team found using the identified effective practice. The remainder of this section describes selected examples of the use of the practice.

Interagency Collaboration

The DoD IC uses DCIPS, an independent system established by legislation in 2004, as part of a broader attempt to standardize IC systems. Under this system, some agencies collaborate on job announcements and applicant sourcing for like positions.[1] Most notably, the Defense Intelligence Agency, NGA, and NSA are working to centralize their hiring by using a single source to post job announcements and providing a single portal through which applicants may apply. The NGA and NSA also establish position requirements by occupation rather than by a specific job and issue a general vacancy announcement. New employees are hired and placed in general "holding" positions to learn about the agency and rotate through different organizations. When an actual position vacancy occurs, immediate placement can be made because a candidate has already been recruited and cleared through the security process.[2]

A DCIPS HR professional explains why this centralized anticipatory hiring practice has been effective: "It may take 150 days [for an applicant] to get through [the] clearance process, but [because of this practice] the manager may only experience a 30-day vacancy."[3] While NAPA conducted an independent evaluation of DCIPS in 2010, the review is now somewhat dated and did not explicitly address hiring and

---

[1] For more on DCIPs, see DCIPS, "Frequently Asked Questions," webpage, April 22, 2011.

[2] Interviews with DCIPS staff members, Telephonic, October 9, 2018 (names withheld on request).

[3] Interview with DCIPS staff member, Telephonic October 9, 2018 (name withheld on request).

Table 4.1
Categorization of Recruiting Effective Practices

Effective Practice	Practice Theme	Practice Category	Agencies That Use Them
Interagency collaborations (e.g., collaborative job announcements and applicant sourcing for like positions among different agencies)	Recruiting flexibilities	Innovative	DCIPS found at National Geospatial-Intelligence Agency (NGA) and National Security Agency (NSA), DoD CES
Video interviewing (e.g., HireVue)	Recruiting flexibilities	Innovative	DCIPS found at the NGA and NSA
Aggressive outreach and DHA (e.g., making job offers at recruiting events)	Recruiting flexibilities	Promising	DCIPS, DoD laboratories, VA
Student employment programs (e.g., job fair outreach and postdoctoral fellowship programs)	Recruiting flexibilities	Innovative	DoD laboratories

recruiting; nor did it raise the issue of centralized anticipatory hiring.[4] Therefore, evidence of the success of this practice appears to be limited to the judgment and experience of DCIPS HR professionals.

Video Interviewing

One change in the hiring process at NGA and NSA has been the implementation of HireVue, an automated application that allows applicants to record their interviews online at any time, allowing hiring managers to access the interviews at their convenience. The use of this kind of technology allows for easier access to applicants and provides managers a record of interviews that they can refer to multiple times, if needed, during the selection process. Applicants are provided with a set of practice questions before recording their interviews with a prerecorded set

---

[4] Edwin Dorn et al., *The Defense Civilian Intelligence Personnel System: An Independent Assessment of Design, Implementation, and Impact*, Washington, D.C.: National Academy of Public Administration, June 2010.

of questions. During the interview, applicants have 30 seconds to prepare for each question and up to three minutes to answer the question.[5]

While the NSA indicated it adopted this automated application based on the NGA's positive experience, the study team was unable to identify any data regarding the effectiveness or efficiency of the automated application.[6]

Aggressive Outreach and Direct-Hire Authority

Both the VA and DCIPS representatives noted the importance of outreach and the use of DHA to make job offers at recruiting events. Under Lab Demo, agencies have several DHAs that allow them to make job offers to science, technology, engineering, and mathematics (STEM) students at recruiting events. There is no USAJOBS notice or formal assessment for this DHA; a manager simply can find a candidate that he or she likes for an open position, and submit the candidate's résumé, transcript, and a qualification statement to the staffing team, which then makes a final qualifications eligibility determination.[7]

Lab Demo DHAs include Hiring Authority for Advanced Degree Candidates, a legislative flexibility enacted in 2009 that allows laboratories to hire master's degree and Ph.D. candidates noncompetitively.[8] Another Lab Demo DHA, Distinguished Scholastic Achievement hiring, allows the labs to direct hire candidates with bachelor's and advanced degrees into STEM positions.

As one representative for the Navy components of Lab Demo noted, "If we can give a contingent job offer early at a career fair, we have the candidate more likely than other organizations that don't have direct hire, so it helps us compete with private industry." [9] In addition,

---

[5]   HireVue, "How to Take a HireVue Interview," webpage, October 7, 2014.

[6]   Interviews with NSA staff members, Telephonic, October 16, 2018 (names withheld on request).

[7]   Interviews with AFRL staff members, Telephonic, October 24, 2018 (names withheld on request).

[8]   Cole, 2012, p. 10.

[9]   Interview with NAVSEA staff members, Telephonic, October 10, 2018.

a 2012 DoD study found that Hiring Authority for Advanced Degree Candidates was an effective tool, but it was underutilized because the Navy did not have a need for the number of advanced degrees authorized under the legislation.[10] However, the study team was unable to identify any more current documentation than 2012 detailing the hiring outcomes associated with this authority.[11]

Student Employment Programs

The DoD laboratories require employees with degrees and experience from STEM fields. To attract a sufficient number of capable candidates, the laboratories participating in Lab Demo have used extensive student employment programs, postdoctoral fellowship programs, job fair outreach, and ongoing relationships with university and college faculty to bolster their recruiting efforts. Through these programs the laboratories are able to reach out to high-quality students and hire them quickly. Further, by having outreach programs at job fairs, the DoD laboratories can directly reach out to minority students, which improves hiring diversity. However, the Lab Demo also indicated that these student outreach efforts have been limited by the Pathways Programs requirement to post job announcements. This requirement limits a hiring manager's ability to quickly select promising students.[12]

Hiring

We identified four effective practices related to hiring, which, along with the agencies that use them, are listed in Table 4.2. The table also identifies the practice theme and category. The narrative that follows provides a description of selected organizations using the practice.

---

[10] Cole, 2012, p. 10.

[11] The most recent evaluation of Lab Demo that could be found was in Cole, 2012.

[12] Cole, 2012, p. 8.

Table 4.2
Categorization of Hiring Effective Practices

Effective Practice	Practice Theme	Practice Category	Agencies That Use Them
DHA managed by organization, not external authorities	DHA	Best	DCIPS, DoD CES, DoD laboratories for certain occupations, FAA, NSA, NIST, USDA ARS, VA Title 38
Three-year probationary period to allow supervisors to make permanent hiring decisions based on employees' demonstrated capabilities	Extended Probationary Period	Best	AcqDemo, CAPS, DoD laboratories, USDA, ARS
Modified veterans' preference	Recruiting Flexibilities	Promising	AcqDemo, DCIPS in NSA, VA, DoD CES, DoD laboratories in AFRL
Student hires placed in more general positions and then advanced to long-term assignments as positions open	Recruiting flexibilities	Innovative	DCIPS in NSA

Direct-Hire Authority Managed by the Organization

In many cases, the study team found that in demonstration projects and APSs, DHA was managed under authorities granted to the individual organizations rather than government-wide authorities. In the Lab Demo, DHA is only for scientists and engineers. Agencies have to fall back on other DHAs provided under 5 U.S.C. for GS employees within the laboratories who are not classified as scientists and engineers.[13] The FAA representative interviewed for the study discussed the FAA's approach to DHA and why it is so useful: "We don't have to go to OPM for requesting DHA. Our lines of business submit busi-

---

[13] Interview with AFRL staff member, Telephonic, October 21, 2018 (name withheld on request).

ness cases and we determine if it meets the qualifications for hard-to-fill (difficulty hiring, offers declined, etc.)."[14] Agency-managed DHA allows for a quicker and targeted response to filling key positions. For more information on DHA, see appendix B.

The Three-Year Probationary Period

When employees are hired into permanent positions, it is sometimes difficult for a supervisor to assess an employee's performance and job fitness within the standard one-year probationary period. When employees are placed into positions with rotations to learn different areas, they are not really performing the tasks required by their permanent position. As a result, managers are unable to evaluate employee performance for a permanent position within that one-year period. Additionally, when jobs require an employee to perform a full-cycle of program that extends over a yearly cycle, there may not be an opportunity to observe the employee's performance at each stage of the cycle.[15] CAPS and the DoD laboratories have been able to overcome these issues by using their authority to create two- or three-year probationary periods to give supervisors more time to make the final appointment decision. While the most recent evaluation of CAPS is dated, it showed that 8 percent of individuals were removed during the second year of probation.[16] This flexibility for an extended two-year probationary period was subsequently implemented across DoD in 2016.[17]

---

[14] Interview with FAA staff member, Telephonic, October 22, 2018 (name withheld on request).

[15] Terry Moon Cronk, "DoD Announces New-Hire Probationary Period," October 3, 2016, U.S. Department of Defense.

[16] Booz Allen Hamilton, *Department of Commerce Personnel Management Demonstration Project Evaluation Year Nine Report*, McLean, Va.: Booz Allen Hamilton, April 15, 2008.

[17] Public Law 114-92, National Defense Authorization Act for FY 2016, Section 1105, Required Probationary Period for New Employees of the Department of Defense, November 25, 2015.

Modified Veterans' Preference

Traditionally, managers were required to select new hires from among the top three candidates referred to them on a hiring certificate. This "Rule of Three" requirement, in turn, was linked to the preference granted to certain military veterans and some family members of veterans. In 2002 the OPM, drawing from a previous demonstrations project, introduced category rating as an option to the Rule of Three. Category rating allows agencies to increase the number of eligible candidates from which a selecting official could choose while preserving veterans' preference rights. This new provision was included in the Chief Human Capital Officers Act of 2002 (Title XIII of the Homeland Security Act of 2002) and codified at 5 U.S.C., Section 3319. In May 2010 a presidential memorandum made the use of category rating mandatory. Over time, a number of agencies received authority for additional modifications to the 5 U.S.C. provisions for veterans' preference and hiring. For example,

- DCIPS applies veterans' preference differently, but only at the point of selection. Veterans need to compete to be included on the "best qualified" list with other job candidates. But once they are on that list, they are likely to be hired.[18]
- The VA applies another variation on veterans' preference; if there are two equally qualified candidates, and one is a veteran and one is not, the veteran gets the job.[19]
- AcqDemo employs veterans' preference but has transitioned its application from choosing based on a points system, as codified in 5 U.S.C., to considering whether the veteran best meets mission requirements.[20]

---

[18] Interviews with DCIPS staff members, Telephonic, October 9, 2018 (names withheld on request).

[19] Interviews with VA staff members, Telephonic, October 25, 2018 (names withheld on request).

[20] Interviews with AcqDemo staff members, Telephonic, October 9, 2018 (names withheld on request).

- The DoD CES applies veterans' preference at the "back end" of selection. Hiring managers decide who to interview, and once they are down to the last two or three candidates, if all are equally qualified, they must select veterans' preference–eligible candidates. If they choose to select a nonveteran, the hiring managers must submit a package to the DoD Under Secretary for Personnel and Readiness to get approval.[21]

- The USDA, ARS does not grant extra points for veterans because it does not assign candidates points or rank numerically. However, all preference-eligible candidates in a group are listed ahead of non-preference-eligible candidates. To pass over any preference-eligible candidates requires approval under formal objection procedures.[22]

- DoC, NIST does not apply veterans' preference for its DHAs. Representatives interviewed said they hire mostly Ph.D.'s and scientists. However, if they did implement veterans' preference for direct hire, they might not have many veterans applying, they noted, because the veteran's candidate pool for their technical positions is small to begin with.[23]

The study team found no data-driven evaluations on the effectiveness of modified veterans' preference. Having data associated with the quality of the applicants under the modified process or the number of veterans who were determined qualified but not selected would have provided more insight on the impact of the process on veteran applicants. Agencies that use modified veterans' preference indicated that they are ensuring that the best qualified applicants get considered rather than placing a veteran on a referral list based on their status and basic qualifications.

---

[21] Interviews with CES staff members, Telephonic, November 8, 2018 (names withheld on request).

[22] 55 Fed. Reg. 9062, U.S. Office of Personnel Management, Agriculture Department, Alternative Personnel Management System: Demonstration Project, March 9, 1990.

[23] Interviews with NIST staff members, Telephonic, October 19, 2018 (names withheld on request).

Student Hires Placed in More General Positions

NSA has a robust student hiring program. They use general open announcements and hire students without placing them in specific positions. As positions become vacant that fit the student's background and interest, they place the student hire into a permanent position. This technique also allows hiring and placing students before completing the full clearance process. The student hires are given work that helps them become familiar with the agency but does not require a high-level security clearance. According to an NSA APS representation, this approach is beneficial because it allows the new employee to get a good sense of the work found in different parts of the agency and also allows the NSA to place a new employee in a position that it thinks is the best fit for the new employee.[24] There have been no evaluations of the NSA's student hire program.

Compensation

The compensation-related effective practices are listed in Table 4.3. The table contains a list of all agencies that the study team found using the identified effective practice. The narrative below the table provides a description of selected organizations using the practice.

Pay Banding

As was discussed in Chapter Two, pay banding was first developed as part of the China Lake demonstration project and allows agencies to collapse the General Schedule 15 grades into a few broad bands with wide salary ranges. Pay banding has two main advantages. First, and most directly relevant to recruiting and hiring, is that it gives managers flexibility to use compensation to recruit and hire professionals with the best skills, as opposed to restricting compensation to a specific grade and step. Second, pay banding allows managers greater latitude to remunerate employees for growth in their current roles, a policy

---

[24] Interviews with NSA staff members, Telephonic, October 16, 2018 (names withheld on request).

Table 4.3
Categorization of Compensation-Related Effective Practices

Effective Practice	Practice Theme	Practice Category	Agencies That Use Them
Pay bands provide flexibilities in placement and discussions with candidates on upward mobility	Pay banding	Best	AcqDemo; CAPS; China Lake; DCIPS; DoD laboratories; DoE NNSA; FAA; all FIRREA agencies, including NCUA; GAO; IRS; NIST; VA
Contribution-based compensation and appraisal system	Contribution-based compensation	Best	AcqDemo, CAPS, DoD laboratories
Advanced in-hire rates without prior approval	Advanced in-hire rates	Promising	Commerce NIST, DoD CES, DoD laboratories in NAVSEA
Checks and balances in the performance management and payout processes to ensure fair treatment of all employees	Pay review and leveling	Best	AcqDemo, DCIPS

that has the potential, in turn, to make the agency more attractive for recruitment and hiring purposes.

Pay banding practices are widely employed across the demonstration projects, APSs, and independent systems. Agencies tend to tailor pay banding practices to their recruitment and retention needs. DCIPS agencies, for example, have the flexibility to use pay banding, but not all make use of the practice. The NGA moved off the GS schedule to a system containing five pay bands to improve talent recruitment and retention; the NSA did not see the need to do so and remains on the GS schedule.[25] Similarly, the CES, the DoD-wide personnel system for cybersecurity professions, does not require the use of pay bands and, in fact, instead organizes employees across three work categories using the GS-15 grade structure; however, the option does exist for agencies

---

[25] For a description of the NGA system, see NGA, "Compensation," webpage, undated.

to develop a pay band structure within these three categories for their cybersecurity workforces.[26]

Pay banding has been evaluated in multiple demonstration projects and personnel systems. Within AcqDemo, pay banding gives managers greater flexibility when setting starting salaries and using compensation for recruitment and retention. A 2016 assessment showed that starting salaries in AcqDemo were approximately $13,000 higher than they were for an equivalent GS population. However, only 26 percent of supervisors believed that AcqDemo had a positive effect on their ability to influence the pay of employees at the time of hiring. Beyond starting salaries, AcqDemo participants earned $1,500 to $1,800 more each year than comparable GS employees in AcqDemo-eligible organizations.[27]

CAPS also uses pay banding for compensation and recruiting. A 2009 study found that 18 percent of employees covered by the broad band system were affected by salary capping, meaning that their salaries were at the maximum for their pay bands despite having performance ratings that could allow them to receive greater compensation.[28] The Lab Demo found similar levels of salary capping, where between 17.8 percent to 20.8 percent of employees in the highest pay band hit the pay ceiling.[29] In evaluations for both programs, we found concerns that salary caps could affect retention—motivating to employees seek employment opportunities elsewhere in order to increase their compensation, but there were no data evaluating this possibility. While pay banding provides managers with increased flexibility in placing employees upon hiring and compensating employees for growth in their current roles, a major drawback has been identified whereby the employees hit a pay ceiling at the top of the band.

---

[26] Interviews with CES staff members, Telephonic, November 8, 2018 (names withheld on request).

[27] Lamping Lewis et al., 2016, p. 60.

[28] Booz Allen Hamilton, 2008.

[29] Cole, 2012, p. 9.

The Contribution-Based Compensation and Appraisal System

Originally developed as part of AcqDemo, the Contribution-Based Compensation and Appraisal System (CCAS) allows federal agencies to tie an employee's compensation to his or her contribution to the overall organizational mission, as opposed to the employee's performance on specific assigned tasks.[30] By rewarding high contributors and withholding pay increases from low contributors, the system aims to attract and retain a highly qualified workforce motivated to maximize its contributions to the organization's mission.[31] The use of the CCAS has since expanded to Lab Demo projects and the CAPS program, as described below.[32]

A 2016 assessment of AcqDemo found that employees with higher levels of contribution to the mission were tied to higher salaries, more promotions, faster salary growth, and improved chance of retention. Specifically, the report showed that AcqDemo employees with strong contributions to the mission could expect to add an additional .4 percent to 1.1 percent to their annual salary growth.[33] The CAPS pay-for-performance system also links performance with salary. A 2009 report showed that covered employees earned more and received larger performance-based bonuses. On average, employees in the CAPS system received a performance-based pay increase of approximately 3.2 percent; the top 13 percent of performers earned salary increases of approximately 6 percent.[34] The use of a contribution assessment to a pay-for-performance employee evaluation adds another distinct method of evaluation that can benefit the top performers in an organization.

---

[30] Lamping Lewis et al., 2016, p. 2.

[31] Lamping Lewis et al., 2016, p. 2.

[32] Interviews with AFRL staff members, Telephonic, October 28, 2018 (names withheld on request); see also Wright-Patterson Air Force Base, "AFRL—Air Force Laboratory Personnel Demonstration Project," webpage, July 8, 2016.

[33] Lamping Lewis et al., 2016, p. xxi.

[34] Booz Allen Hamilton, 2008.

While some demonstration projects' performance appraisal systems can successfully link compensation to performance, employees might not fully appreciate this connection. Evaluations have shown that multiple programs, such as the CCASs used by AcqDemo and the DoC, which tie employee performance to compensation, employees often indicate that they do not understand this link, and thus often doubt its validity.[35] Agencies need to address the disconnect between the perceived and actual effects of appraisal systems to foster employee trust and understanding of system changes.

Advanced In-Hire Rates

Advanced in-hire rates allow agency managers some flexibly to set compensation during hiring without having to receive prior approval. For example, NAVSEA Warfare Centers, which are part of Lab Demo, have the flexibility to start employee salaries anywhere within a pay band. Many NAVSEA Warfare Centers set entry-level science and engineering salaries at the top of the pay band, which is equivalent to GS-8 to GS-10 pay rates.[36] Similarly, NIST has a pay band system that allows managers to set initial pay anywhere within the relevant band.[37] The ability to use and immediately effect advance in-hire rates has the benefit of improving the time to recruit, as well as the ability to pay a higher starting salary to quality candidates who might otherwise go with a competitor who can offer higher pay.

Checks and Balances on Performance Management and Payout Processes

Performance-based compensation systems require consistent evaluations of employees to ensure fairness. Given that some organizations with such systems have employees who do not see the connection between their contributions and their compensation, organizations

---

[35] Lamping Lewis et al., 2016, p. xx; Booz Allen Hamilton, 2008.

[36] Interviews with NAVSEA staff members, Telephonic, October 10, 2018 (names withheld on request).

[37] Interviews with NIST staff members, Telephonic, October 19, 2018 (names withheld on request).

should be concerned with how their performance-based systems are implemented. DCIPS uses a system of checks and balances to evaluate the fairness of its performance management and payout processes. This system is supported by two key roles: the reviewing official and the Performance Management Performance Review Authority (PM PRA).

The reviewing official evaluates the review ratings created by subordinate rating officials and ensures that they are compliant with DCIPS policies and guidelines. If the official disagrees with the ratings, the official discusses the discrepancy with the rating official who submitted the review. The reviewing official may change the review rating if he or she feels that it was not determined fairly or was not compliant with DCIPS guidelines. The PM PRA is senior to the reviewing official and evaluates all the reviews for fairness and compliance with DCIPS policies and guidelines. DCIPS also has a Pay Pool Performance Review Authority to ensure the fairness of the pay pool process. The Pay Pool Performance Review Authority comprises DoD intelligence component heads, who have final authority for pay pool recommendations.[38]

This system allows employees to use an appeals process, where ratings and pay decisions can be reevaluated if they appear unfair. The PM PRA can examine an employee's rating upon request, and employees can also go to the DoD component head if they are dissatisfied with their PM PRA's decision. While DCIPS employees cannot challenge their individual compensation, they can file grievances on the pay pool process. The implementation of a system with checks and balances provides double benefits. First, it ensures that the system is being used as designed, and second, it increases transparency of the process allowing employees to see how the process works and does not favor one type of employee over another.

---

[38] Dorn et al., 2010.

Crosscutting Practices

The study team identified a number of issues that cut across the reviewed organizations but did not necessarily meet the standards for effective practices. We considered these issues worthy of inclusion because they assisted multiple organizations to more effectively and productively implement or operate their APS or demonstration project.

Publishing and Disseminating Rules, Policies, and Information

Demonstration projects and APSs that publish and disseminate the rules, policies, and information for their systems are able to improve understanding and awareness of the systems components and what they are trying to achieve. In a review of the of AcqDemo, it was found that subject matter experts spoke favorably of the communication and feedback mechanisms.[39] The use of effective communications was also found in the FAA and in DoE, NNSA.

Allowing Union Employees to Opt In

The full benefit of implementing the flexibilities and innovations found in demonstration projects and APSs cannot be realized when unions prevent the opportunity to extend flexibilities to employees who are covered by a bargaining unit agreement. This problem has been recognized since the inception of the first demonstration project. At its Rome, New York, location, the AFRL has worked effectively with the union to develop a compromise. Union employees can decide if they want to join the Lab Demo or not, which allows employees who would like to join the demonstration project to exercise this option. In using this approach, organizations that have bargaining unit employees can increase the number of employees covered by the demonstration project or APS. Union employees participating can then share their experiences and potentially convince other union employees to join the demonstration project or APS.

---

[39] Lamping Lewis et al., 2016.

Opportunities to Improve Evaluation Processes and the Implementation of Results

Our review of program evaluations and interviews with federal HR representatives helped us not only identify effective practices related to developing and implementing demonstration projects and APSs, as discussed in Chapter Five, but also *revealed a number of evaluation process and implementation shortfalls*—issues associated with specification, conduct, oversight, and reporting of evaluation outcomes, as well as implementation of the demonstration projects and APSs themselves. During our interviews, federal HR representatives explained that deficits in the evaluation process make it difficult to sufficiently assess effective practices within an agency for greater consideration by leadership and to support and inform broader generalizations and design improvements to programs in other agencies.

Our study did not explicitly set out to identify process improvements, but the topic frequently arose during our interview discussions about effective practices. As we shared results of our research with the project sponsor, the sponsor expressed interest in understanding process and implementation shortfalls so that DoD (and potentially the OPM and the broader federal HR community) could consider them in a more comprehensive context associated with continuous process improvement. The sponsor acknowledged that federal and agency responsibilities in these process areas have changed over time, and in some areas this has resulted in insufficient or inconsistent requirements specification and voids in accountability. Therefore, our sponsor requested that we document such observations and offer considerations for review by DoD and the broader HR community.

Because we did not rigorously or systematically analyze process issues, we offer only general observations and possible considerations that DoD and other federal agencies may explore further. Before DoD takes action on these observations, there is need for

- more rigorous examination of the operational context (for both DoD and other federal agencies) in which observations are noted and considerations are offered
- identification of appropriate and specific DoD, OPM, and governance structures or federal forums to develop, manage, and oversee plans and actions
- designation of offices with primary responsibility for taking action or leadership
- further assessment as to whether considerations can be accomplished within the given authorities of an agency or whether additional legislative action is required
- greater review of the advantages and disadvantages of each consideration, which would also include estimates of costs for implementation.

The perspectives of federal executives—collected primarily through interviews—highlighted four areas where evaluation process and implementation shortfalls pose challenges. We discuss these four areas along with considerations for potential resolution in the remainder of this chapter. The four areas are

1. **Specifying evaluation standards.** Committing to rigorous and transparent evaluation processes that define standards, retain data, and publicly disseminate evaluation results.
2. **Determining and implementing effective practices.** Empowering existing or modified governance structures that provide intra- and interagency oversight of evaluation design, execution, reporting, and broader implementation, if warranted.

3. **Overcoming roadblocks to HR change.** Sufficiently defining requirements and providing adequate resources needed for program specification, implementation, and change management; also including consideration of key stakeholder perspectives.

4. **Reducing HR system complexity.** Explicitly considering and seeking to balance unintended consequences associated with program proliferation against the difficulties of program understanding, administration, and management.

Specifying Evaluation Standards

There Is No Central Authority or Standards for Data Collection

Title 5 of the U.S.C., Chapter 47, requires the OPM to provide guidance and foster innovation in federal HR management, which includes responsibilities for evaluating demonstration projects and APSs. Based on our legislative authorities review, the OPM's responsibilities for the evaluation process vary based on whether the program is a demonstration project or an APS.[1] However, we learned through our interviews that the OPM is not currently engaged in such responsibilities, though it did oversee and gather such information until 2008.[2] The

---

[1] For demonstration projects that are under OPM auspices, see U.S. Code, Title 5, Chapter 47, Section 4703 (b)(1)(H), Demonstration Projects, January 3, 2012; C.F.R., Title 5, Part 470, Subpart C, Section 470.301; and OPM, 1999. When an APS is established under separate legislative authority, there is no OPM-prescribed evaluation process or required evaluation elements; however, the authorizing legislation may provide evaluation guidance. For example, legislation specifically mandated assessment criteria for the AcqDemo project; see Lamping Lewis et al., 2016. Finally, the FY 2019 NDAA outlined requirements for each agency with a demonstration project to submit an annual report to the OPM, the Office of Management and Budget, and the Committee on Oversight and Government Reform of the House of Representatives. Specific reporting requirements were detailed in Public Law 115-232, John S. McCain National Defense Authorization Act for Fiscal Year 2019, August 13, 2018.

[2] Between 2005 and 2008, the OPM issued four annual reports on the demonstration projects and APSs, thereby fulfilling the role intended in 5 U.S.C. to support research and innovation in federal HR. These reports reinforced the federal government's experience for improving key systems that are critical to the strategic management of human capital, emphasized the use of information about APSs in making future HR restructuring decisions,

HR executives with whom we spoke further explained that, for unde-termined reasons, the OPM stopped performing these responsibilities after 2008 and did not implement another mechanism requiring such information despite emphasizing the importance of shared program evaluations in an earlier publication.[3] Based on our review of directive language and authorities, the study team was unable to find a central authority actively engaged in identifying evaluation requirements and data standards today.

Interviewees also emphasized that with no requirement to col-lect evaluative data against appropriate standards for demonstration projects and APSs, most agencies do not engage in ongoing or system-atic efforts to collect data on outcomes. The net result has been that a number of the effective practices for hiring, recruiting, and compensat-ing the federal civilian workforce has either never been evaluated or do not have consistent evaluations to determine their effectiveness. Our interviewees also noted that such difficulties have led to a lack of pro-gram accountability, an inability to assess the need for program modi-fication, and lack of essential information to inform agency leader-ship in their decisionmaking processes. The RAND team's experience aligns with these observations because we found only eight program evaluations to use in our assessment of effective practices.

From our perspective, one way to reenergize today's stagnant eval-uation process is to establish a forum where interagency representa-tives can collaborate in identifying a uniform set of evaluative data and standards that should be collected and analyzed for every dem-onstration project and APS.[4] When identifying data requirements and standards, it will be necessary to take into account the differences in project design and innovations being pursued in the various demon-

---

and reaffirmed the need for a government-wide data source for information associated with demonstration projects and APSs.

[3] OPM, 2007.

[4] This consideration does not necessitate the creation of a new body but rather charges an appropriate authority for the oversight, conduct, and assessment of these assigned roles and responsibilities. The same is true for other considerations that reference an interagency forum.

stration projects and APSs and build in sufficient flexibility to account for those differences—similar to the varying evaluation approaches in the *Demonstration Projects Evaluation Handbook*.[5] Extending data collection requirements to pilots and other alternative systems would help ensure effective practices from those efforts are also shared. It is also important to factor the requirements outlined in the FY 2019 NDAA into the development of a uniform set of data.[6]

There Is No Central Repository of Evaluation Outcomes

Title 5 of the U.S.C., Chapter 47 charges the OPM to "establish and maintain a program for the collection and public dissemination of information relating to personnel management research and for encouraging and facilitating the exchange of information among interested persons or entities."[7] We learned from our interviews that the OPM—despite sufficient authority—is not maintaining evaluation data or outcomes to facilitate systematic analysis across agencies for program generalizations and extensions.

While HR pilots were not the subject of this study, in our discussions with federal HR executives we uncovered a number of such programs that are authorized by legislation to operate outside of 5 U.S.C. for a specific predesignated time frame. Pilots can in effect create new pay systems, new appointment authorities, and new HR systems that will contain similar flexibilities provided in demonstration projects and APSs that deviate from the requirements found in 5 U.S.C. Interviewees noted that pilots should be included in any data-gathering requirements in the same way as the demonstration projects and APSs.

To facilitate collection and retention of evaluation outcomes, we believe a successful approach would be to establish a publicly available central repository of information regarding each demonstration project

---

[5] *Demonstration Projects Evaluation Handbook*, U.S. Office of Personnel Management, April 1, 1999.

[6] Public Law 115-232, 2018.

[7] U.S. Code, Title 5, Chapter 47, Section 4702, Research Programs, January 3, 2012.

or APS. This repository would contain descriptions of the flexibilities that were implemented, innovations tested, program outcomes, evaluation reports, and findings—including data from other alternative systems, such as pilot programs. All agencies could contribute data and have access to the information so they can share and learn from the posted effective practices.

Determining and Implementing Effective Practices

No Standards Are Used for Determining Effective Practices

Based on our interviews and literature review, the study team found no evidence of government- or agency-wide standards for identifying effective practices for HR innovations that might become candidates for implementation across the government. Interviewed executives reported anecdotal success with some initiatives, but they noted that standard data regarding the impact of hiring, recruiting, and related compensation reforms were scarce. They attempted to identify practices that they considered "best," but acknowledged that there was no definitive or established criteria used to assess the collection of practices and associated outcomes.

To develop standards for defining effective practices, we offer that an interagency forum should consider developing standards for determining effective practices. The group should focus on a range of methods and criteria that can be used to determine effectiveness. The method applied in this study and the criteria detailed in Table 1.1 could serve as a starting point.

No Mechanism Exists to Consider Effective Practices for Broader Implementation

During our interviews we also learned that there was no requirement for agencies to systematically consider practice outcomes of other agencies as they sought to design and implement appropriate flexibilities for their own workforce. The deficiencies in evaluative standards, data, and repositories mentioned earlier inhibits this process. However, the lack of such collaboration and cross-agency sharing of information for broader government enactment is counter to the OPM's accounts in reports issued in 2005–2008.

Other than informal coordination among agencies, the study team was not able to document (either through interviews or literature reviews) systematic processes for cross-agency sharing of practices (to include pay for performance, relocation bonuses, category ratings, and recruitment incentives). When questioned about the most effective flexibilities, the HR executives we spoke to most frequently mentioned pay banding, followed by DHA under agency authority. Despite readily available responses concerning practice effectiveness, the interviewees' replies were inconsistent as to how information from such practices was shared among their federal HR colleagues for possible broader implementation.

Based on the HR experiences of the study team, we believe if sharing mechanisms were in place, individual agencies could benefit from the experiences of other agencies who are experimenting with similar concepts, and could make better decisions regarding their own practices that should be improved, modified, or even canceled. Similarly, agencies either individually or collectively could work to advance practices across the three stages of effectiveness defined in previous chapters—from innovative to promising to best. Toward that end, we offer that an interagency forum could establish and implement an appropriate mechanism through which effective practices and outcomes from demonstration projects and APSs would routinely be examined for broader adaption by other agencies.

In our view, such a mechanism should be based on existing executive governance bodies, executed as an ongoing requirement and focus area, and augmented by functional expertise or other process stakeholders on an as-needed basis. This structure would serve in an executive cross-agency capacity in which the aforementioned considerations would be addressed, overarching policy and guidance would be promulgated and monitored, and agencies would report against established standards and outcome metrics. We believe that individual agencies should be free to consider this information and be empowered to design and modify program features consistent with their workforce specifics and regulatory authorities. The 14 effective practices identified in Chapter Four could serve as a starting point for this interagency mechanism and allow individual agencies to conduct the necessary due diligence to determine applicability to their circumstances.

Overcoming Roadblocks to Human Resources Change

Our interviewees reported a number of obstacles to establishing agency-level reforms of personnel, recruiting, and associated compensation. Our analysis of the many obstacles raised points to two primary impediments (additional topics were mentioned, just not consistently): the amount of time and resources needed for executing significant HR change, and complexities associated with union engagement.

Insufficient Resources to Assess and Implement HR Change

The HR executives we interviewed said that agencies must invest considerable time and resources to research appropriate and needed flexibilities, determine effective and relevant practices, design and/or tailor program specifics to their agency situations, estimate overall program costs, and identify possible unintended outcomes (and even secondary/tertiary effects). They lamented that these actions must be addressed before even the basics associated with a change management initiative can be instituted—for example, leadership engagement, strategic communications, and training development and delivery.

Our interviewees noted that such comprehensive analysis and preparatory actions are typically the antithesis of agency leadership's preferences and desired time frames. Leadership emphasis is frequently placed on achieving "quick wins," an elusive concept in the complex HR arena. The precursory actions are not only essential to implementation success but take considerable time to work through and properly construct. For example, the study team found that the new DoD CES authority is programmed for a design and implementation period of over seven years before all employees are transferred into the new system. While the authority was part of the FY 2017 NDAA, the system is not projected to be fully implemented until 2024.

Many agency HR professionals—the basis for our interview sample—realize that these time and resource constraints are necessary to ensure that employees' equities and interests are sufficiently considered, addressed, and protected. Unfortunately, they cited many occasions in which adequate resources are not available to support the required workload. Or, in the cases where resources are initially available, the executives commented that resources are not sustained over time to complete even the basic complement of necessary actions. They stated that as a consequence of limited resources, agencies are often deterred from pursuing HR flexibilities that likely are needed to address workforce challenges.

If agencies budget for the necessary time to research effective practices and ensure that there are sufficient resources to support the workload that is required for design, implementation, and evaluation, we think that HR staffs would be more likely to pursue effective flexibilities. We believe that when all planning consideration are scoped and supported, agencies will be able to consider successful and unsuccessful HR programs that have already been implemented and apply truly best and appropriate practices to support their agency mission and strategic needs (and possibly achieve some economies).

Complexities Associated with Union Engagement

Title 5 of the U.S.C. specifies that employees located within an organization that is accorded exclusive union recognition cannot be included in a demonstration project unless certain conditions apply, such as

- if the project would violate a collective bargaining agreement, unless there is another written agreement with respect to the project between the agency and the organization permitting the inclusion
- if the project is not covered by such a collective bargaining agreement, until there has been consultation or negotiation, as appropriate, by the agency with the labor organization.[8]

---

[8]   U.S. Code, Title 5, Part III, Subpart C, Chapter 47, Section 4702 (f), Demonstration Projects, January 12, 2018.

Based on these conditions, demonstration projects and APSs are not considered fully implemented until the entire workforce is included. Our discussions with agency HR professionals found that it takes considerable time for union employees to transition into such programs—if they ever do. Accordingly, organizations are required to operate multiple HR systems to serve their diverse workforces. Interviewees noted that the complexity of the rules increases dramatically in such circumstances, making it difficult for HR professionals, supervisors, managers, and even employees to understand which rules pertain to which employees and in what situations.

The study team found through its literature review that a majority of demonstration projects do not cover union employees because of these 5 U.S.C. provisions. However, we learned from our interviews that the AFRL in Rome, New York, has started to effectively engage union employees by allowing employees covered by a collective bargaining agreement to individually decide on an annual basis whether to "opt in" to the program. Because of this innovative practice, union member participation in the laboratory demonstration project has been steadily increasing. HR professionals said they negotiated the opt-in approach so that union employees could determine how the CCAS was working for their peers, and then decide whether they wished to participate. Other AFRL demonstration project sites are considering implementing this practice at their worksites.

We suggest that one way to address the issues of union engagement is to establish an interagency forum to collaborate with the OPM to determine how to engage positively with the unions to participate in program justification, design, implementation, and, ultimately, the participation of its members. Demonstration project and APS implementation often requires difficult negotiations with unions, and, in many cases, bargaining unit employees are not being included in the new system. This results in a bifurcated workforce with different personnel processes and potentially different personnel conditions (e.g., differing compensation levels for comparable employees within the same organization). In addition, it increases the complexity for managers who must use the systems, as well as HR professionals who must manage and administer multiple systems. The innovative approach successfully implemented by AFRL may provide agencies and union personnel with a degree of flexibility to address both organizational needs and individual preferences.

Reducing Human Resources System Complexity

We found through our literature review that personnel systems have proliferated across the federal government in recent years. Our interviews confirmed that the myriad of changes to 5 U.S.C. have made it difficult for HR professionals to understand and stay abreast of recruiting, hiring, and related compensation legislative and policy options. The study team found that there are currently 20 agency demonstration projects, 21 APSs, and six government-wide DHAs covering over 24 occupational series. In DoD there are an additional 11 DHAs (from the last four NDAAs) covering over 29 different occupational series. Some DHAs are focused on specific subcomponents of the workforce. For DoD financial management positions, the authority is limited to 10 percent of the total number of finance, accounting, management, actuarial science, or financial management positions. This restriction is further complicated in that it is applied within each DoD component, based on positions filled as of the close of the fiscal year (not always a precise number). For select DoD acquisition positions, the authority is limited to 1 percent of the total number of scientific and engineering positions within the acquisition workforce of that military department.

Our interviewees explained that all of these authorities created a complex web of legislation and policy guidance that makes the jobs of HR professionals more complex and increases the probability of errors in implementation. HR professionals who support organizations with multiple systems and authorities must understand the associated rules and regulations. Interviewees also pointed out that limited or no training is available on the nuances of the multitude of HR programs (including hiring alternatives) for either HR professionals or managers.

Furthermore, in accordance with OPM government-wide rules for DHA approval and use, respondents commented that there are a number of requirements, such as public notice, that can substantially delay recruitment and hiring. They stated that the requirement for posting does not allow for immediate job offers at job fairs and other hiring events, a feature that other companies are able to exploit to their advantage in the competitive hiring process.

Based on these HR complexities and actionable items consistently mentioned in our interviews, the study team offers the following actions for further development and consideration.

First, consolidate DHAs to simplify occupations covered, standardize the amount of time the authority is available, and allow for agency administration. The 11 DoD DHAs, referenced above, cover 29 occupations and have six different end dates. HR executives explained that such complexity does not contribute to greater organizational success or enhanced employee engagement, and they thereby call for a simplification of processes and return to "first principles."

Second, assess restrictions associated with the DHA public notice requirement in USAJOBS and propose alternatives for critical occupations. Interviewees stated that targeted implementation of streamlined hiring practices would allow their organizations to be more competitive for high-demand skills.

Third, assess available training for HR professionals and managers and provide training to address critical gaps. Interviewees consistently suggested that agencies need to develop and sufficiently fund additional training for federal government HR professionals. This would include creating information resources on the nuances of the different federal HR systems and how such programs can be used effectively to maximize mission support.

Examining Clearance Factors in Hiring Delays

Several other factors outside the purview of HR and unrelated to demonstration projects or APSs were frequently raised in our interviews as influencing the federal government's ability to hire employees effectively. Interviewees repeatedly mentioned that suitability determinations and security clearance requirements delay the hiring process. Such delays threaten the government's ability to hire the most qualified and desired candidates, who cannot or will not wait for the time it takes to clear both of these hurdles. Respondents commented that even when a demonstration project or APS shortens federal agencies' historically lengthy hiring timelines, suitability and security requirements can still significantly delay appointments. We offer that these clearance factors are worthy of additional investigation to determine whether changes to the processes can accelerate the hiring process without compromising suitability and security requirements.

CHAPTER 6

Conclusion

The history of demonstration projects and APSs provides a stark illustration of the complex political, bureaucratic, and economic factors that have shaped the U.S. government's federal HR system. While the OPM played a central role in launching the original personnel demonstration projects, its relatively conservative approach, as well as legal and policy constraints, have led several federal agencies to pursue alternative legislative and policy paths to adopt personnel management reforms outside the purview of 5 U.S.C. The proliferation of personnel management reforms outside of 5 U.S.C. have allowed agencies to tailor HR flexibilities to their specific HR needs. However, these reforms also have contributed to the complex web of law, policies, and procedures that managers and HR professionals must navigate to recruit, hire, and compensate quality personnel.

In this report, the study team examined the outcomes of the various demonstration projects and APSs. While evaluations and interviews provided insights into potential effective practices, we could find no standard definition of what constitutes an HR best practice. Despite this shortcoming, the study team judged that many of the identified effective practices could be used to inform the establishment of future independent systems or, indeed, government-wide HR reforms.

The identification of effective practices, as well as observations and considerations found for the evaluation process, can inform the government's direction as it addresses the need for a talented and high-performing workforce supported by contemporary and effective HR systems and practices. These considerations can be critical to modernizing and refining current HR programs, as well as to the design and implementation of programs for new organizations, such as DoD's merged commissary and exchange organization or the DoD U.S. Space Force. They also support DoD and the OPM in achieving CAP subgoal 3, developing a workforce for the twenty-first century.

Descriptions of Demonstration Projects and Alternative Personnel Systems

In support of the DASD(CPP) response to the PMA, this study collected information on all federal government initiatives related to HR demonstration projects and APSs. We restricted our time horizon from the present day back to the last major status report of such work published by the OPM, in 2008.[1] We limited our compilation to initiatives that are specifically focused on recruiting, hiring, and related compensation practices. This appendix only includes programs that are still functioning as of May 2019, omitting any that have ceased to operate (e.g., PACER SHARE and the NSPS). We organize our compilation into four major groupings: agency managed demonstration projects, APSs that were former demonstration projects, other independent personnel systems, and programs within financial regulatory agencies.

As discussed in the body of this report, the research team attempted to collect complete and publicly available information detailing these HR initiatives. The ultimate goal was to assemble published evaluations. To the extent that such documentation was not available or did not exist, we pursued other means. We started this process by connecting with the responsible and cognizant officials at the OPM. We sought access to federal or agency information that may not be readily available to the public (e.g., contracted evaluations conducted by external companies), as well as agency-specific contacts who could possibly provide internally produced papers. We also conducted a wide

---

[1] OPM, 2007.

range of internet and database searches attempting to discover information on any of the ongoing programs. We systematically reviewed FRNs over time to assemble programmatic issues, changes, and intent associated with particular initiatives. This work also included a review of the respective codes and titles applicable to departments or agencies for which we were only able to gather limited information. Finally, to supplement these methods, we also conducted agency interviews. Based on the interview protocol (which is reproduced in Appendix C), we sought to capture as much information about an agency's program in terms of the impetus for its development, specific policy and process changes, the impact of such changes, and the documentation of findings and recommendations.

This appendix provides a brief overview of each HR initiative that satisfies the above criteria. Table 3.1 provided an overall synopsis by highlighting key information and showing areas where we were not able to collect relevant data. For each initiative, we highlight the flexibilities that were desired as a result of its implementation.

Agency-Managed Demonstration Projects

The Civilian Acquisition Workforce Personnel Demonstration Project

AcqDemo began in 1999 as an opportunity to reengineer the civilian personnel system to meet the needs of DoD's Acquisition, Technology and Logistics workforce and to facilitate its ability to fulfill the department's acquisition mission. The project provides for managerial control over personnel processes and functions and uses retention, recognition, and rewards to support the professional and personal growth of employees. One project goal is to improve recruitment, hiring, and compensation flexibilities to aid the development of the DoD workforce.[2]

---

[2]   64 Fed. Reg. 1426, U.S. Department of Defense; Civilian Acquisition Workforce Personnel Demonstration Project, January 8, 1999.

While the OPM originally approved the demonstration, it now falls under the authority of the Secretary of Defense.[3] AcqDemo has adopted several of the authorities found in early demonstration projects such as pay banding, simplified classification and hiring processes, and expanded probationary periods for new hires in some positions. Most recently, AcqDemo implemented four new DHAs for acquisition student interns, business and technical management positions, veterans, and individuals with scholastic achievements. AcqDemo has also implemented the Voluntary Emeritus program, which allows the DoD to accept voluntary service. Veterans' preference has not changed significantly, but its application has shifted from selection based on a "total points" system to considering the veteran who best meets mission requirements.

The CCAS was developed under this demonstration project; it links employee compensation to contribution to the mission, which is measured differently from overall performance, and establishes a structured group review process to assess employee contributions to mission and performance quality. The CCAS rewards high contributors and aims to attract qualified, motivated candidates to work in DoD.[4]

AcqDemo has undergone multiple modifications over the years. Recent changes include reducing the six classification and appraisal factors to three, establishing DHAs, expanding the supervisory probationary period, expanding detail and temporary promotion authority, and revising reduction-in-force procedures, among several other changes.[5] While AcqDemo has been operating for 20 years, it is still a demonstration, with a current expiration date of 2023. However, AcqDemo has continuously received five-year extensions. Absent legislation to make it permanent, we anticipate that it will continue.

DoD maintains an up-to-date website that describes AcqDemo and its ongoing modifications, extensions, and evaluations (http:// acqdemo.hci.mil). The study team found and used a number of assess-

---

[3]   82 Fed. Reg. 52104, Department of Defense, Civilian Acquisition Workforce Personnel Demonstration (AcqDemo) Project, November 9, 2017.

[4]   Lamping Lewis et al., 2016.

[5]   82 Fed. Reg. 52104, 2017.

ments beginning with a Baseline/Implementation Evaluation Report in 2000 and, most recently, a 2016 assessment conducted by RAND.

The Department of Defense Science and Technology Reinvention Laboratory Personnel Management Demonstration Project

The FY 1995 NDAA gave the Secretary of Defense the authority to develop personnel demonstration projects at various DoD STRLs (also referred to as Lab Demo) with the approval of the OPM. These demonstration projects were designed to improve the recruitment, hiring, and compensation systems for employees at the various labs.[6] While the demonstration projects follow many of the same requirements of 5 U.S.C., Chapter 47, the FY 1995 NDAA, Section 342, removed a limitation for employees covered, as well as a mandatory expiration date. The FY 2001 NDAA gave sole responsibility of these demonstration projects to the Secretary of Defense. While the STRLs are covered by the demonstration project authority, each laboratory was required to publish an approved demonstration project plan in an FRN. As of May 2019, there are currently 18 Lab Demo projects:

- There are 11 in the U.S. Department of the Army:
  - Armament Research, Development, and Engineering Center
  - Army Engineer Research and Development Center
  - Army Medical Research and Materiel Command
  - Army Research Institute
  - Army Research Laboratory
  - Army Research, Development, and Engineering Command: Edgewood Chemical Biological Center
  - Aviation and Missile Research, Development, and Engineering Center
  - Communications-Electronics Research, Development, and Engineering Center
  - Natick Soldier Research, Development and Engineering Center
  - Space and Missile Defense Command Technical Center

---

6   Public Law 103-337, Section 342(b).

- Tank Automotive Research, Development and Engineering Center
- There are six in the U.S. Department of the Navy:
  - Naval Air Warfare Center, Naval Air Systems Command Weapons and Aircraft Divisions
  - Naval Facilities Engineering and Expeditionary Warfare Center
  - Naval Research Laboratory
  - NAVSEA Naval Surface Warfare Center
  - Office of Naval Research
  - Space and Naval Warfare Systems Command, Weapons Division and Aircraft Division
- There is one in the U.S. Department of the Air Force:
  - AFRL

While each laboratory has created internal procedures and operates with some autonomy, they share many commonalities and are all affected by certain statutory amendments that are universal, such as hiring authorities, delegated classification authority, and pay banding. Overall, Lab Demo uses many flexibilities found in other projects. For example, laboratories have DHAs for science and engineering positions, as well as for students from STEM programs. While laboratories adhere to OPM qualification standards, they are not required to use USAJOBS to advertise position vacancies. The laboratories also use pay banding, and new employees' pay can be set anywhere within the pay band.

As an example, the Naval Surface Warfare Center demonstration project began in 1998.[7] The original goal of the project was to improve the recruitment and retention of scientists and engineers. In terms of hiring, the Naval Surface Warfare Center uses DHAs for employees with bachelor's or advanced degrees, military veterans in STEM fields, and STEM graduates. It also uses DHA for financial management positions, secondary school students, recent graduates, and for posi-

---

[7] 62 Fed. Reg. 64050, U.S. Office of Personnel Management, Science and Technology Reinvention Laboratory Personnel Demonstration Project at the Naval Sea Systems Command Warfare Centers, December 3, 1997.

tions at selected installations. Students with a grade point average of 3.5 or higher can also be hired under a DHA using the Distinguished Scholastic Achievement authority. For compensation, managers have delegated classification authority, and a pay band system is in place that uses pay for performance.

Each laboratory may have multiple organizations operating in more than one location. The AFRL is a good example of this diversity of staff and location, as it has eight technology directorates, one wing, and one office located in five different states, with over 10,000 military and civilian personnel. The geographic dispersion and different organizational missions add to the complexity of implementing and managing a demonstration project.

The Department of Energy's National Nuclear Security Administration

The NNSA began its personnel demonstration project in 2007, after receiving OPM approval. The focus of the project was to attract top talent, which was deemed particularly necessary in an organization that requires a large number of STEM-related positions.[8] The demonstration project features a pay banding system, simplified position classification, and various hiring processes beyond those found in the GS system, including the use of DHAs, and veterans' preference is not required. Within the project, compensation is tied to performance, where high performers receive an increase in pay while poor performers do not. The FY 2018 NDAA extended the demonstration project for ten more years.[9]

---

[8] OPM, "Personnel Demonstration Project; Pay Banding and Performance-Based Pay Adjustments with the National Nuclear Security Administration," *Federal Register*, Vol. 72, No. 245, December 21, 2007, pp. 72776–72802

[9] Public Law 115-91, Title VIII, Subtitle D, Provisions Relating to Acquisition Workforce, Section 844, Extension and Modifications to Acquisition Demonstration Project, December 12, 2017.

Alternative Personnel Systems That Are Former Demonstration Projects

The Department of the Navy's Navy China Lake Demonstration

In Public Law 103-337, Section 342, the expiration date for the Navy China Lake Demonstration was removed, thus creating the first permanent APS from a 5 U.S.C. demonstration project.[10] The original demonstration project was implemented in 1980 with the purpose of expanding managerial control over personnel functions, creating a more responsible personnel system, and creating an integrated approach to pay, performance, and classification.[11] To accomplish these goals, China Lake used several interventions.

First, the demonstration project introduced the concept of "pay banding," in which employees were able to be paid outside of the traditional GS system. Instead of positions being slotted within one of the 15 grades of the GS system, China Lake classified them into one of the five pay bands. In this new system, multiple grades were combined into a single band, which allowed a greater range of salaries for any one position. Employees in this system could be paid more or less than in the traditional GS system, and supervisors were able to have more control over compensation. Supervisors were also to develop performance plans with the goal of effectively communicating employee responsibilities and supervisor expectations. In addition, supervisors were instructed to conduct two progress reviews at the fifth and ninth months of the performance cycle. Employees were encouraged to list their accomplishments for these progress reviews. China Lake also permitted reduction-in-force procedures that aimed to increase retention of the most capable employees. This involved ranking the employees, first by their performance and then by their retention standings.

---

[10] Public Law 103-337, National Defense Authorization Act for Fiscal Year 1995, Title III, Subtitle C, Section 342, Extension and Expansion of Authority to Conduct Personnel Demonstration Projects, October 5, 1994.

[11] OPM, "Proposed Demonstration Project: An Integrated Approach to Pay, Performance Appraisal, and Position Classification for More Effective Operation of Government Organizations," Federal Register, Vol. 45, No. 77, April 18, 1980, pp. 26504–26544.

China Lake's performance appraisal and performance-linked pay interventions were both met with positive responses from employees. Reports at the time noted that employees were satisfied with the changes to supervision, performance appraisal, and the promotion opportunities provided by those changes.[12] These positive responses helped propel the China Lake demonstration project into becoming a permanent APS.

As one the earliest APSs, China Lake is often cited as a pioneer on which many other programs are based. The study team was able to find only one publicly available evaluation of the system, a 1988 GAO report. The examination was in response to a congressional request and focused on how relevant the project was to the proposed Defense Industry and Technology Act of 1988.[13] The lack of evaluations for China Lake is most likely due to its age and few documented changes over the years.

The Department of Commerce's National Institute of Standards and Technology

In 1986, the OPM and NIST were given the authority to jointly design an alternative personnel management system demonstration project under Public Law 99-574.[14] They designed the demonstration project to improve the hiring process through DHA, the use of higher entry salaries, and various recruiting allowances. These abilities would also allow NIST to be a more attractive employer for high-quality researchers. In addition, the demonstration project would give NIST the opportunity to improve retention through pay banding, a pay-for-performance system that allowed for higher pay potentials, and

---

[12] OPM, Research and Demonstration Staff, *Navy Personnel Management Demonstration Project: The Effects of Performance Based Pay on Employee Attitudes*, Washington, D.C.: U.S. Office of Personnel Management, Management Report IV, June 1985.

[13] GAO, *Federal Personnel: Observations on the Navy's Personnel Management Demonstration Project*, Washington, D.C.: U.S. Government Accountability Office, GGD-88-79, May 3, 1988.

[14] Public Law 99-574, National Bureau of Standards Authorization Act for Fiscal Year 1987, October 28, 1986.

an improved managerial system of personnel management. The public law outlined specific features of the demonstration project, including pay banding, a new performance appraisal system, and recruitment allowances. In 1987 the demonstration project received final approval with the features outlined in the public law.[15] Since then NIST's system has evolved and undergone multiple amendments and alterations.

Despite these changes, however, NIST still follows the goals of the 1986 public law. As such, the current APS has DHAs for all technical staff and for a few nonprofessional technical positions. It also uses a pay band system through which managers can set the initial pay anywhere within a band. This works hand in hand with the pay-for-performance system, through which employees are rated on a seven-level system that affects how much employees are paid within their bands. Public Law 104-113, the National Technology Transfer and Advancement Act of 1995, Section 10, Personnel, extended NIST's alternative personnel management system indefinitely, thus making it a permanent APS.

The study team searched for evaluations for NIST through the FRNs detailing modifications to the system and through NIST's website. A 1996 evaluation from the OPM titled *Summative Evaluation Report National Institute of Standards and Technology Demonstration: 1998–1995* has been cited in a 2012 FRN, but the study team was unable to find a copy.[16] In an interview, a NIST representative noted that the DoC conducts an annual audit of the system, as well as a Human Capital Accountability Framework audit every three years. However, the interviewee also noted that the OPM review was the most substantive.

---

[15] 52 Fed. Reg. 37096, Office of Personnel Management, Personnel Demonstration Project, Alternative Personnel Management System at the National Bureau of Standards, October 2, 1987.

[16] 77 Fed. Reg. 48128, National Institute of Standards and Technology, Alternative Personnel Management System (APMS) at the National Institute of Standards and Technology, August 13, 2012.

The Department of Commerce's Alternative Personnel System

After NIST's demonstration project was made permanent in 1996, the DoC designed a project that sought to test if NIST's interventions would work in different DoC environments.[17] As this project was based on NIST, it has the same goals and contains the same interventions: simplified position classification, pay for performance, and simplified recruiting and examining processes. The DoC's demonstration project began in 1998 with 2,800 employees across four DoC organizations. By 2003 the demonstration project had expanded to include employees from eight more DoC organizations and had undergone several modifications. The project was extended in 2003 to last another five years. In 2007 the Consolidated Appropriations Act made the demonstration project a permanent system, and it was then renamed the Commerce Alternative Personnel System (CAPS). The program has continued to undergo changes, most of which have been to expand CAPS to other DoC organizations.[18]

The DoC engaged Booz Allen Hamilton to conduct annual evaluations on CAPS, which are readily available on the agency's website.[19] These evaluations cover the first nine years of the project (2000–2008) and examine the effectiveness of the project, as well as provide recommendations. While it is not known why these annual evaluations ceased, they were the only ones the study team found for CAPS. If DoC continues to conduct annual audits of the system like NIST, they have not been made publicly available.

---

[17] 62 Fed. Reg. 67434, U.S. Office of Personnel Management, Personnel Demonstration Project, Alternative Personnel Management System for the U.S. Department of Commerce, December 24, 1997.

[18] 82 Fed. Reg. 1688, Department of Commerce, Commerce Alternative Personnel System, January 6, 2017.

[19] U.S. Department of Commerce Office of Human Resource Management, "Commerce Alternative Personnel System (CAPS)," webpage, undated.

The Department of Agriculture's Agricultural Research Service

The USDA proposed a demonstration project for ARS in an August 23, 1989 FRN.[20] Originally the USDA wanted to create a staffing system that would improve the hiring process to attract and attain high quality employees. The demonstration project's first innovations were to "decentralize the decision for DHA in shortage categories, utilize categorical ratings instead of numeric scores, provide an option of monetary incentives for recruitment purposes, and reimburse relocation/travel expenses beyond those authorized."[21] In 1998, the demonstration project became a permanent APS with the passage of Public Law 105-277.

The study team was told that in a 2014 memorandum from the headquarters of the USDA, many of the authorities and flexibilities available for all positions within ARS were restricted to research scientists. Initially, the demonstration project used DHA for all positions, but it can now be used only for research scientists within ARS. All other positions use delegated examining authority. ARS also uses department-wide promotion authorities along with those found in 5 U.S.C. (such as Pathways, and Schedule A for hiring new employees from outside the government). In terms of the recruitment of research scientists, ARS is authorized to use recruitment, travel, and transportation incentives for their new hires. New research scientists can receive reimbursement for house hunting, relocation services, and the sale of a residence. The APS also removes the 5 U.S.C. cap for cash payments for recruitment incentives or bonuses. Standard position descriptions are used for all positions aside from research scientists, who must use very specific descriptions.

---

[20] 54 Fed. Reg. 35135, U.S. Office of Personnel Management, Proposed Demonstration Project, Department of Agriculture, August 23, 1989.

[21] 55 Fed. Reg. 9062, 1990.

Other Independent Personnel Systems Created Outside Title 5 of the U.S. Code

Some agencies have been granted by independent statutes the authority to create and implement their own independent personnel systems outside of 5 U.S.C. These systems do not count against the OPM's limit for demonstration projects and were established by agency-specific laws or authorities.

The Department of Transportation's Federal Aviation Administration

The 1996 DoT Appropriations Act gave the FAA authority to establish an APS that would be separate from 5 U.S.C. provisions. Unlike other systems, the FAA's APS did not start as a demonstration project, and was launched without a pilot period. The goal of the APS was to improve hiring flexibility and employee placement to better compete with the airline industry. The APS also aimed to change the compensation system to one using pay banding and pay for performance. The FAA uses DHA for certain positions, such as mission critical occupations and for individuals with targeted disabilities. The FAA can operate without OPM oversight, and DHA is possible without OPM approval. However, FAA policy limits the usage to certain situations such as hiring for hard-to-fill positions. Congress can also affect hiring (e.g., the FAA Extension, Safety, and Security Act of 2016, which changed the hiring process for air traffic control specialists).[22] Aside from hiring, the FAA also uses pay banding, and managers are delegated classification.

The FAA's APS has been evaluated multiple times, and the study team was able to find evaluations and GAO reports covering the system. Most recently, NAPA completed an in-depth assessment on the effectiveness of FAA's system.[23]

---

[22] Public Law 114-190, Title II, Subtitle A, Safety, Section 2106, Hiring of Air Traffic Controllers, July 15, 2016.

[23] Jonathan Breul, John Palguta, and Nancy Potok, *Federal Aviation Administration: Personnel Reform Effectiveness Assessment*, Washington, D.C.: National Academy of Public Administration, January 2017.

The Department of the Treasury's Internal Revenue Service

In 1998 the IRS Restructuring and Reform Act was established to create pay systems that were different from the GS system.[24] Working with the OPM, the IRS developed criteria for the new pay system, which included incorporating the grades and steps of the GS pay system into the new system. With its newfound authority, the IRS developed the IRS Payband System, a pay-for-performance system that covers IRS managers below the executive level. Employees within the system receive pay increases that result from performance ratings. When IRS employees are promoted to either a temporary or permanent management position, they are placed in the pay band and are eligible for a onetime pay increase based on their experience. Such a pay increase is based on the employee's base pay, in addition to locality pay.[25]

Along with authorizing the IRS to develop a new pay system, the IRS Restructuring and Reform Act also created the Treasury Inspector General for Tax Administration (TIGTA), which is responsible for conducting audits and evaluations of IRS operations, including human capital procedures. As a result, TIGTA published several evaluations of the IRS's pay system. These evaluations were found on the TIGTA's website, which contains archives of their audits and finding assessments of the IRS's pay system.

The Government Accountability Office

GAO has had a long history of using an APS. In 1980, the GAO Personnel Act authorized GAO to implement a pay-for-performance pay band system for specialists and analysts.[26] One original goal of the new pay band system was to better reward employees for their knowl-

---

[24] Public Law 105-206, Internal Revenue Service Restructuring and Reform Act of 1998, July 22, 1998.

[25] Treasury Inspector General for Tax Administration, *Some Managerial Salaries Were Calculated Incorrectly Due to Complex Pay-Setting Rules,* Washington, D.C.: Treasury Inspector General for Tax Administration, 2017-10-023, March 29, 2017.

[26] Public Law 96-191, General Accounting Office Personnel Act of 1980, February 15, 1980.

edge and performance instead of only tenure within the office.[27] The office was also granted certain Comptroller General DHAs for up to 15 experts and consultants. This was used for select cases in positions that needed to be filled quickly.

The Personnel Flexibilities Act of 2000 and the GAO Human Capital Reform Act of 2004 granted more authorities to the office and ushered in new changes to GAO's personnel system.[28] The 2000 act was designed to reduce the number of high-grade supervisory positions without reducing the overall number of GAO employees. The legislation authorized GAO to make voluntary early retirement offers to certain employee groups, create senior level positions with compensation and benefits in line with Senior Executive Service positions, and give greater consideration for employee performance and knowledge when making reduction-in-force actions.

The Human Capital Reform Act further expanded GAO authorities. Under this Act, GAO was able to make the early retirement offer authority permanent, allowed for greater reimbursements for relocation, increased the amount of leave for employees and officers with less than three years of public service, created an exchange program with private sector, and established a market-sensitive pay banding compensation system. The act allowed for the pay rates for GAO employees to be based on the market and gave the comptroller authority to determine pay increases in accordance with the budget.[29]

Section 11 of the GAO Human Capital Reform Act of 2004 required GAO to provide a final report and assessment no later than six years after the act was enacted. This final report was used in the research for the present report.

---

[27] GAO, *Human Capital Flexibilities*, Washington, D.C.: U.S. Government Accountability Office, GAO-02-1050R, August 9, 2002.

[28] GAO, *Final Report on GAO's Use of Provisions in the GAO Human Capital Reform Act of 2004*, Washington, D.C.: U.S. Government Accountability Office, GAO-10-811SP, July 6, 2010.

[29] James R. Thompson, *Designing and Implementing Performance-Oriented Payband Systems*, Washington, D.C.: IBM Center for the Business of Government, 2007.

The Department of Homeland Security's Transportation Security Administration

The Aviation and Transportation Security Act created the TSA in 2001.[30] Section 114 of the act gave the Under Secretary of Homeland Security authority to create modifications to the TSA's personnel management system. The legislation provided the TSA the ability to apply the personnel management system established for the FAA, allowing TSA leadership to make such modifications to the personnel management system as appropriate. In 2006, the TSA debuted its new pay-for-performance system, the Performance Accountability and Standards System (PASS), which aimed to place more emphasis on workplace performance and accountability. PASS was designed to be a transparent system in which employees would have the ability to learn about performance metrics that affect their compensation and the overall mission of the TSA.[31] The system used pay banding and provided financial rewards for remarkable performance. Employee performance was measured through performance on the job and through scores on a certification test. PASS was canceled and superseded by the Transportation Officer Performance System in March 2013.[32] As a result of controversy surrounding the subjectivity and fairness of the certification tests, employee competency is now solely assessed by the quality of job performance.[33]

The Consolidated Appropriations Act of 2008 required the TSA to submit a report to Congress on the implementation of PASS. That report was made publicly available and was referenced for the present

---

[30] Public Law 107-71, Aviation and Transportation Security Act, November 19, 2001.

[31] TSA, *The Transportation Security Administration's Report to Congress on the Implementation of the Performance Accountability and Standards System (PASS) for the 2007 Performance Cycle*, Washington, D.C.: Transportation Security Administration, May 2008.

[32] Transportation Security Administration Management Directive No. 1100.73-4, Reasonable Accommodation Program, Washington, D.C.: Transportation Security Administration, September 3, 2018.

[33] Federal Soup, "TSA Pact Scraps Pay-For-Performance System," webpage, August 10, 2012.

report. However, the research team was unable to find a record of an evaluation for the Transportation Officer Performance System.

The Defense Civilian Intelligence Personnel System

The FY 1996 NDAA gave the IC the authority to create a mission-focused personnel system that allowed for greater flexibility in hiring employees. The program, DCIPS, was based on policies from the Army that could be applied to the IC.[34] While DCIPS was authorized in 1996, it would not be fully implemented for nearly a decade. There was little attention paid to the program until after the events of 9/11, which shifted the mission of the IC, as well as the organizational structure. In the FY 2003 NDAA, the position of Under Secretary of Defense for Intelligence was created. With the enacting of the Intelligence Reform and Terrorism Prevention Act in 2004, the Director of National Intelligence was formed. Together these clear authorities combined to create a system each of the intelligence agencies could use for their personnel system.

In 2006 the IC launched a Pay Modernization Feasibility Study conducted by the NSA. The study examined the IC and other innovations in pay modernization throughout the federal government in order to view potential improvements to HR management. The study concluded that the IC would benefit from developing a central architecture "throughout the community that would contain a central framework of processes for civilian compensation.[35] This led to the creation of the National Intelligence Civilian Compensation Program, which aimed to create a central framework for compensation for all employees within the IC. This would not be a single system, but instead a collection of systems with common goals and procedures. The goal of the National Intelligence Civilian Compensation Program was to "enable

---

[34] DCIPS, "About DCIPS," webpage, undated.

[35] Improving Performance: A Review of Pay-for-Performance Systems in the Federal Government: Hearing Before the Subcommittee on Oversight of Government Management, the Federal Workforce, and the District of Columbia, 110 Cong. 814 (2009) (Statement of Ronald Sanders).

the IC to recruit, motivate, and retain highly qualified individuals" for intelligence activities.[36]

NAPA prepared an independent assessment of DCIPS in 2010 and submitted the report to Congress and DoD.[37] An interview with an IC representative confirmed that this was the only publicly available external evaluation.

While the NSA is part of the DCIPS system, it is important to note its use of flexibilities and the fact that the NSA system began before the establishment of DCIPS. The NSA is a unique government agency because it was never intended to be an agency within 5 U.S.C.[38] However, the NSA's HR system shares several features found in other demonstration projects and APSs. The NSA uses DHA, where candidates are evaluated against minimum qualification standards and the vacancy of the job. The agency aims to reduce vacancies as much as possible, with the goal of having 98–100 percent of jobs filled at the end of each fiscal year.[39] The NSA does have the flexibility to implement pay banding, but has chosen to continue to use the standard GS grades and steps. Approximately 70 percent of the NSA staff are on the standard GS pay schedule, while the remaining staff are on special salary schedules. The staff on these special salary schedules are mainly those in STEM-focused positions, police officers, and polygraphers. The NSA also uses relocation and recruitment incentives.

The research team did not find any records of publicly available evaluations of the NSA's flexibilities. However, officials from the IC and the NSA discussed the existence of internal reviews.

---

[36] Intelligence Community Directive No. 650, *National Civilian Compensation Program: Guiding Principles and Framework*, Washington, D.C.: Officer of the Director of National Intelligence, April 28, 2008.

[37] Dorn et al., 2010.

[38] Public Law 86-36, National Security Agency Act of 1959, May 29, 1959.

[39] Interviews with NSA staff members, Telephonic, October 10, 2018 (names withheld on request).

The Department of Defense's Cyber Excepted Service

DoD continues to develop its new HR system, the CES, in order to better support the unique mission and workforce of the Cyber Command and the department's cybersecurity workforce. Congress gave the Secretary of Defense the authority to create this system in FY 2016 under Title 10 of the U.S.C., Section 1599f.[40] The goals of the CES are to give more effective flexibilities for recruiting and retaining cybersecurity professionals, create agile recruitment options for high-quality candidates, streamline hiring procedures in order to quickly acquire talent, and develop a pay structure that could compete with other jobs in the market.[41] The Office of the Chief Information Officer oversees the CES while the Office of the Under Secretary of Defense for Personnel and Readiness leads the implementation of the system. While the CES is permanent, it will continue to grow; the first two phases of rollout will affect anywhere from 3,000 to 5,000 employees.

The GS grading structure, with 15 grades, each having ten steps, is used for CES positions. Managers have the authority to place individuals on their initial appointment anywhere between steps 1 and 10 in the grading system. The CES has established two additional steps in the grading system, but managers must obtain higher-level approval to use the top two steps. Hiring managers can make job offers on the spot at various career fairs. The CES does not use a pay band system, but instead will implement a graded rank and position structure. However, components can submit proposals for a pay band structure that could be implemented with approval from the Office of the Chief Information Officer and the Office of Under Secretary of Defense for Personnel and Readiness. At the time this report was written, the CES was still relatively new, and it will be undergoing more changes as it expands and grows. The study team was told, in an interview with a CES representative, that the CES did not perform a baseline assessment but had performed a Phase 1 evaluation with lessons learned, site

---

[40] U.S. Code, Title 10, Subtitle A, Part II, Chapter 81, Civilian Employees, Section 1599f, November 25, 2015.

[41] Defense Civilian Personnel Advisory Service, *Cyber Excepted Service: Frequently Asked Questions*, Washington, D.C.: Defense Civilian Personnel Advisory Service, January 2018.

visits, questionnaires, training course evaluations, investment score-cards, and the semiannual reporting requirements.[42] This evaluation was not provided to the study team.

The Department of Homeland Security's Cyber Excepted Service

DHS was authorized under Public Law 113-277, the Border Patrol Agent Pay Reform Act of 2014, to establish an excepted service HR system for its cybersecurity workforce. Under the provisions of the statute, the department has the authority to establish an HR system with the ability to establish positions, appoint an individual, and fix compensation in the excepted service. It also has the authority to use a three-year probationary period. DHS is still developing its CES system and specific details are not available.

The Department of Veterans Affairs

The VA has three different authorities that it operates under: 5 U.S.C., Title 38 of the U.S.C., and a hybrid of 5 U.S.C. and Title 38. For purely Title 38 occupations (medical or related fields), the VA has its own noncompetitive hiring authorities. As long as individuals have qualifications and certifications, the VA can hire them, and then they go before a board of their peers to set their pay. The VA does not have to post job announcements, but it often advertises positions in journals as a means of outreach and recruiting, especially for more rural areas. For hybrid positions, the same thing applies, but the VA has a labor agreement that requires that it post job announcements for hybrid positions, even though it is not required by law. The announcements are typically open for 14 days, first internally and then externally (a bargaining unit requirement). The VA does apply veterans' preference in that if it has two equal candidates and one is a veteran and the other is not, the veteran is selected. In 2013 there was a Merit Systems Protection Board decision that the VA must apply veterans' preference for

---

[42] Interview with CES staff member, November 11, 2018 (name withheld on request).

the hybrid positions the way the rest of the government does under 5 U.S.C.[43] The study team was unable to find an evaluation.

Financial Regulatory Agencies

FIRREA was enacted in the wake of the savings and loan crisis of the 1980s. When launched, it was considered a bailout for failed savings and loan banks, but it has become a powerful antifraud tool to prosecute banks making intentionally bad loans.

FIRREA and the Dodd-Frank Act of 2010 granted federal financial agencies the flexibility to establish their own compensation systems to enhance their ability to recruit and retain employees critical to meeting organizational mission needs. Congress also directed agencies to seek to maintain pay comparability and to consult with each other in doing so to ensure the agencies do not compete with each other for employees. Today, financial reform and enforcement agencies include

- the CFPB
- the Commodity Futures Trading Commission
- the Farm Credit Administration
- the Federal Deposit Insurance Corporation
- the Federal Housing Finance Agency (note: the Housing and Economic Recovery Act of 2008 combined the Office of Federal Housing Enterprise Oversight and the Federal Housing Finance Board to form the Federal Housing Finance Agency)
- the NCUA
- the OCC
- the Office of Financial Research
- the Securities and Exchange Commission.

In 2007 GAO analyzed FIRREA agency performance management and pay system guidance and procedures; it also interviewed key

---

[43] Interview with VA staff member, October 25, 2018 (name withheld on request).

agency officials and union representatives, focusing on six key performance management practices:

1. aligning individual performance expectations with organizational goals
2. connecting performance expectations to crosscutting goals
3. using competencies to provide a fuller assessment of performance
4. linking pay to individual and organizational performance
5. making meaningful distinctions in performance
6. involving employees and stakeholders to gain ownership of performance management systems.

According to its 2007 Report, GAO found that the agencies implemented key performance management practices in ways that consider organizational cultures and structures. GAO also reported that the agencies had opportunities to refine their systems. For example, at the time of the GAO report, the Commodity Futures Trading Commission and the Securities and Exchange Commission gave across-the-board salary increases even to employees who received unacceptable performance ratings. That is no longer the practice. GAO also found that the agencies had opportunities to improve both processes and communication. The study also concluded that the FIRREA comparability provision and similar provisions in later laws have been effective in ensuring general compensation comparability between the agencies.[44]

Individual FIRREA agencies evaluate their programs, often using contractors as evaluators. We were unable to obtain the evaluations, which generally are not publicly available.

Like the other financial regulatory agencies, the NCUA was granted the authority to establish a separate HR system through the passage of FIRREA in 1989. The NCUA has flexibilities for pay, benefits, and classification. FIRREA dictates that the financial regula-

---

[44] GAO, *Financial Regulators—Agencies Have Implemented Key Performance Management Practices, but Opportunities for Improvement Exist*, Washington, D.C.: U.S. Government Accountability Office, GAO-07-678, June 2007.

tory agencies must coordinate flexibilities with each other in order to prevent competition between the agencies. Currently the NCUA does not have DHA and uses the same hiring authorities as the rest of the government. For compensation, NCUA has an enhanced 401(k), enhanced dental and vision insurance coverage, and an NCUA savings plan. The NCUA also has a Health Examining Program whereby the organization will pay for medical services not covered by insurance. While the salaries within the NCUA are not competitive with those in the private sector, these other benefits are designed to make the NCUA more attractive to potential employees. The NCUA uses some 5 U.S.C. recruiting incentives, including relocation incentives, but does not use student loan repayment. The organization can also set higher pay for entry-level positions and set higher locality rates than agencies covered by the GS system. These compensation flexibilities and benefits are all intended to help recruit top talent.[45]

---

[45] Interview with NCUA staff member, Telephonic, October 26, 2018 (name withheld on request).

Direct-Hire Authorities

Many federal agencies seek to improve the recruitment and hiring process by using DHAs. Agencies can use a DHA in three ways: employing a government-wide DHA as established by the OPM (see Table B.1); seeking OPM approval for a DHA, per 5 C.F.R. 337; or using a DHA granted via a specific legislation establishing an APS. Generally, a DHA is established when it is determined that there is a severe shortage of candidates or a critical hiring need.

Notably, in the cases when public notice is still required, DHA can expedite the hiring process by eliminating competitive ranking and rating, veterans' preference, and Rule of Three procedures. The ability of agencies to use DHA for certain occupations has expanded recently. In October of 2018 the OPM added additional STEM and cybersecurity occupations to the government-wide DHA list. The FY 2017 NDAA, Section 1139, provides DHA for certain federal wage positions throughout the government. Table B.1 presents an analysis of government-wide DHAs.

In addition to specific government-wide DHA granted by the OPM, agencies, including DoD, have also sought legislation to improve student and recent graduate hiring within their own ranks. For example, under the provisions of the 2019 NDAA, DoD may hire a limited number of recent college graduates in a streamlined fashion similar to a DHA.[1] In recent years, DoD has requested a number of DHAs

---

[1] Jeff Neal, "Why Hiring Reforms in the 2019 NDAA May Not Make a Difference," Fed-Smith.com, August 16, 2018.

Table B.1
OPM Government-wide Direct-Hire Authorities

Coverage	Coverage	Expiration
Medical Occupations: Diagnostic Radiologic Technologist, GS-0647; Medical Officer, GS-0602; Nurse, GS-0610, GS-0620; Pharmacist, GS-0660	All grade levels at all locations for the listed occupations.	None given
IT Management: 2210	For positions GS-9 and above at all locations.	Indefinitely or until OPM terminates
Veterinary Medical Officers	For positions GS-1 through GS-15 grade levels (or equivalent) nationwide, to include overseas territories and commonwealths including Puerto Rico, Guam, and the Virgin Islands.	Indefinitely or until OPM terminates
STEM positions: Economist, 110; Biological Science, 401; Fishery Biologist, 482; General Engineer, 801; Civil Engineer, 810; Physical Sciences, 1301, 1306, 1310, 1320; Actuary, 1510; Mathematics, 1520; Mathematical Statistician and Statistician, 1529, 1530; Acquisition, 1102	For positions at the GS-11 through GS-15 grade levels (or equivalent) nationwide, for enabling simple and strategic hiring to attract top talent and to create a workforce for the twenty-first century where a severe shortage or critical hiring need has been identified. These appointments are subject to public notice requirements in 5 UCS 3327 and 3330 and 5 C.F.R. 330, as well as procedures in 5 C.F.R. 330 pertaining to candidates' eligibility for priority selection, and requirements in 5 C.F.R.332.402.	October 10, 2023
Cybersecurity-related positions: Computer Engineers (Cybersecurity), (854); Computer Scientist (Cybersecurity), 1550; Electronics Engineers (Cybersecurity), 855; IT Cybersecurity Specialist (2210)	For cybersecurity-related positions GS-11 through GS-15 grade levels (or equivalent) nationwide, for enabling simple and strategic hiring to attract top talent to create a workforce for the twenty-first century where a severe shortage or critical hiring need has been identified. These appointments are subject to public notice requirements in 5 UCS 3327 and 3330 and 5 C.F.R. 330, as well as procedures in 5 C.F.R. 330 pertaining to candidates' eligibility for priority selection, and requirements in 5 C.F.R. 332.402.	Indefinitely or until OPM terminates

Table B.1—Continued

Coverage	Coverage	Expiration
Federal Wage Schedule Employees	The Director of OPM shall permit an agency with delegated examining authority under 1104(a)(2) of 5 U.S.C. to use DHA under Section 3304(a)(3) for permanent or nonpermanent positions in the competitive service at GS-15 (or equivalent) or below, or for prevailing rate employees if the OPM determines that there is either a severe shortage of candidates or a critical hiring need.	None given

to improve recruitment and hiring for key occupations and students. Over the last four fiscal year NDAAs, DoD was authorized 11 different DHAs with different coverage and expiration dates, as outlined in Table B.2.

Use of Direct-Hire Authorities

In general, the main HR focus areas for demonstration projects and APSs have been on compensation and employee performance, and not specifically on the utilization of a DHA. As noted earlier in this report, by using compensation and pay banding, many agencies are more competitive in recruiting and retaining top talent. According to the OPM and our interviews, this has allowed agencies to improve recruiting and retention at DoD Lab Demo and the Alcohol and Tobacco Tax and Trade Bureau.

Almost all of the agencies we interviewed used some form of DHA to meet their hiring needs. In most cases, these are government-wide DHAs. However, there are a number of agency-specific delegations for DHAs. In the past, DoD specifically included the authority for the Secretary of Defense to approve DHAs, rather than the OPM, as in under the NSPS in 2009. Generally, the Secretary of Defense would follow similar procedures with respect to determining a critical hiring need or severe shortage. While the NSPS was repealed, the inclusion of a DHA provision was clearly meant to address the agency needs for attracting top talent. Under the AcqDemo, a number of DHAs were rolled out for student interns, business and technical management, veterans, and scholastic achievement.[2]

In our interviews, we found that DHAs, when used appropriately, can be a critical step in improving the hiring process. However, inefficient internal processes, lengthy security and suitability requirements, compensation, and private-sector competition can also affect the ability of agencies to recruit and hire top talent.

---

[2] Interviews with AcqDemo staff members, Telephonic, October 9, 2018 (names withheld on request).

Table B.2
Department of Defense Direct-Hire Authorities from FY 2016 Through FY 2019

Coverage	Coverage	Expiration
NDAA FY 2016, Section 1112: DHAs for select technical acquisition positions (qualified veteran candidates for STEM positions, including technicians into the defense acquisition workforce)	Secretary of Defense may carry out a pilot program to assess the feasibility and advisability of appointing qualified veteran candidates to positions in the defense acquisition workforce of the military departments without regard to the provisions of 5 U.S.C., Chapter 33, Subchapter 1. Authority is limited to 1% of the total number of scientific and engineering positions within the acquisition workforce of that military department.	November 22, 2020
NDAA FY 2016, Section 1113: DHAs for select technical acquisition positions (qualified candidates possessing a scientific or engineering degree directly related to scientific and engineering positions within the defense acquisition workforce)	Each secretary of a military department may appoint qualified candidates possessing a scientific or an engineering degree to scientific and engineering positions within the defense acquisition workforce without regard to the provisions of 5 U.S.C., Chapter 33, Subchapter 1. Authority is limited to 5% of the total number of scientific and engineering positions within the acquisition workforce of that military department.	December 31, 2020
NDAA FY 2017, Section 1106: DHA for DoD for postsecondary students and recent graduates	Provides DoD with on-campus recruiting authority under Title 10 as an alternative to the federal government-wide Pathways program (established by Executive Order 13562) and other 5 U.S.C. hiring authorities. Requires DoD to provide public notice and advertising of positions offered under this authority.	September 30, 2025

Table B.2—Continued

Coverage	Coverage	Expiration
NDAA FY 2017, Section 1110: DHA for financial management experts in the DoD workforce	Secretary of a military department provided direct appointment authority to appoint qualified candidates possessing a finance, accounting, management, business administration, or actuarial science degree to financial management, accounting, auditing, and actuarial positions within the DoD workforce. The authority is limited to 10% of the total number of finance, accounting, management, actuarial science, or financial management positions within each military department that are filled as of the close of the fiscal year last ending before the start of such calendar year.	December 31, 2022
NDAA FY 2017, Section 1125: Temporary DHA for Domestic Defense Industrial Base facilities, the Major Range and Test Facility Base, and the Office of the Director of Operational Test and Evaluation	Provides directors of DoD test and evaluations facilities the same DHAs already provided to the directors of the department's science and technology laboratories. DHA for DoD industrial base facilities located in the United States, as well as the Major Range and Test Facility Base.	September 30, 2021
NDAA FY 2017, Section 1105b: Noncompetitive temporary and term appointments to meet critical hiring needs in DoD DHA for shortage category and/or critical need positions	Secretary of Defense may make a temporary appointment or a term appointment (one to five years) in the department when the need for the services of an employee in the department is not permanent. If there is a critical hiring need, the Secretary of Defense may make a noncompetitive temporary appointment or a noncompetitive term appointment in the DoD without regard to the requirements of 5 U.S.C., Sections 3327 and 3330, for a period that is not more than 18 months.	N/A

Table B.2—Continued

Coverage	Coverage	Expiration
NDAA FY 2017, Section 1104: Public-Private Talent Exchange	Secretary of Defense has the authority to arrange for the temporary assignment of an employee to such private-sector organization, or from such private-sector organization, to a DoD organization under this section. An assignment under this section shall be for a period of not less than three months and not more than two years, renewable up to a total of four years.	N/A
NDAA FY 2017, Section 1122: Codification and modification of certain authorities for certain positions at DoD research and engineering laboratories	The director of any STRL may appoint qualified candidates possessing a bachelor's degree; qualified veteran candidates to positions; or qualified candidates enrolled in a program of undergraduate or graduate instruction leading to a bachelor's or an advanced degree in a scientific, technical, engineering, or mathematical course of study at an institution of higher education as an employee in a laboratory described in that paragraph without regard to the provisions of 5 U.S.C., Chapter 33, Subchapter 1 (other than Sections 3303 and 3328 of such title). The appointment authority under Subsection 1 cannot exceed 6%, 3%, and 10% (respectively) of the total number of scientific and engineering positions in such laboratory that are filled as of the close of the fiscal year last ending before the start of such calendar year.	N/A
NDAA FY 2018 Section 559: DHA for DoD for child care services providers for department child development centers	The Secretary of Defense may appoint, without regard to any provision of 5 U.S.C., Chapter 33, Subchapter 1, qualified child care service providers in the competitive service if the secretary determines that there is a critical hiring need for child care service providers for DoD child development centers, and there is a shortage of child care service providers.	September 30, 2021

Table B.2—Continued

Coverage	Coverage	Expiration
NDAA FY 2018, Section 1101: DHA for the DoD for personnel to assist in business transformation and management innovation	The Secretary of Defense may appoint in the DoD individuals described in Subsection (b) without regard to the provisions of 5 U.S.C., Chapter 33, Subchapter 1, for the purpose of assisting and facilitating the efforts of the department in business transformation and management innovation. The individuals described in this subsection are individuals who have all of the following: (1) A management or business background; (2) experience working with large or complex organizations; (3) expertise in management and organizational change, data analytics, or business process design. The number of individuals appointed at any one time may not exceed ten. Any appointment under this section shall be on a term basis and shall be subject to the term appointment regulations in 5 C.F.R. 316 (other than requirements in such regulations relating to competitive hiring). The term of any such appointment shall be specified by the secretary at the time of the appointment.	September 30, 2021
NDAA FY 2019, Section 1101: DHA for certain competitive service positions	Title 5 of the U.S.C., Chapter 99, is amended by adding at the end of the following Section 9905 DHAs for certain personnel for the DoD. The Secretary of Defense may appoint, without regard to the provisions of Chapter 33, Subchapter 1 (other than Sections 3303 and 3328 of such chapter), qualified candidates to any of the following positions in the competitive service of the DoD: • Department Maintenance Act activities, including depot maintenance and repairs • Cybersecurity • Acquisition workforce that manages any services contracts necessary to the operation and maintenance of programs • Any science, technology, or engineering position, including any such positions at the Major Range and Test Facility Base	September 20, 2025

Interview Protocol

We are from the RAND Corporation, a nonprofit policy research organization, and we are conducting a Department of Defense (DoD)–sponsored project to assist the Deputy Assistant Secretary of Defense for Civilian Personnel Policy in fulfilling DoD's obligation, as a partner with the U.S. Office of Personnel Management, to address the President's Management Agenda cross-agency priority (CAP) Goal focused on developing a workforce for the 21st century and specifically the Subgoal associated with simple and strategic hiring. The Workforce CAP Goal also includes an initial set of key strategies and milestones through FY19. This project supports Subgoal 3 strategies that aim to make it easier to recruit top talent, reduce the hiring cycle timeline, and improve the applicant assessment. DoD has specific responsibilities for two milestones, one of which is: "Examine best practices of Federal demonstration projects and alternative personnel systems." As part of this effort, we are interviewing senior leaders, officials, and/or subject-matter experts from organizations and agencies that have or have had personnel demonstration projects or alternative personnel systems.

We have asked you to take part in a roughly one-hour interview based on your position, experience, and/or expertise. During the interview we will ask you a series of questions on your organization or agency's personnel flexibilities associated with a demonstration project or alternative personnel system (defined for this study to mean a personnel system that operates outside the boundaries of the general Title 5 system under OPM oversight), specifically focusing on hiring and compensation. We will use the information you provide to assist DoD in responding to the PMA task by developing a catalog of demonstration projects and alternative systems, document-

ing the reviews of those systems and identifying the best practices and lessons learned from demonstration projects or alternative personnel systems. We will minimize the potential for your responses to harm your reputation and/or employability by not attributing your statements to you in any of our reports or other deliverables. Additionally, we will not disclose details of your participation without your permission except as required by law. Lastly, we will maintain strict separation between your private/personally identifiable information and your interview responses during storage and transmission.

Your participation in this interview is voluntary. The RAND study team will not report refusals to participate and will not document such refusals in project archives. You have the right to refuse to answer any question and may terminate participation at any time after the interview begins. Your input, however, is critical to accomplishing Subgoal 3 under the President's Management Agenda, and we encourage you to share as much as possible.

Interview Questions
1. When did your Demo Project or APS begin?
    a. If the Demo has been ongoing for a long time—Have you or will you seek authority to make the Demo permanent?
    b. For APS only if Demo was made permanent—Were there any effects from the Demo becoming permanent?
2. What was the reason for requesting Demo authority or seeking legislative change for your APS?
3. What hiring policies and processes (direct hire, direct examining, category rating, etc.) do you currently employ? Are these covered by demonstration project or APS authority or by Title 5 authorities?
    a. If hiring policies and processes are under Demo or APS— What impact have these changes had on your ability to locate and hire quality candidates?
    b. If hiring policies and processes are not under Demo or APS—What were the decision points in staying with Title 5 hiring policies processes?

4. What compensation policies and processes (delegated classification, simplified position description [PD], standard PDs, etc.) do you currently employ? Are these covered by demonstration project or APS authority or by Title 5 authorities?
   a. If compensation policies and processes are under Demo or APS—What impact have these changes had on your ability to locate and hire quality candidates?
   b. If compensation policies and processes are not under Demo or APS—What were the decision points in staying with Title 5 hiring policies processes?
5. Have you completed process improvement studies on recruitment and hiring, and if so—What process did you use (for example, Lean) and what did you find and improve?
6. Which human capital policies or process changes were most successful/effective? (Note to interviewer: this question goes beyond hiring and compensation if the interviewee has suggestions.)
7. Which human capital policies or process changes were unsuccessful/ineffective? (Note to interviewer: this question goes beyond hiring and compensation if the interviewee has suggestions.)
8. What human capital changes did you implement that made the biggest impact?
9. What are the lessons learned that you would like to share with others?
10. What evaluations have been made on your demonstration project or APS?
    a. What organization conducted reviews?
    b. When were the evaluations conducted?
    c. What were the significant findings?
    d. Can we obtain a copy of the evaluation(s)?
11. Do you track the effectiveness (ex: quality of hires, timeliness in filling vacancies, performance of new hires) of your recruitment and hiring efforts?
12. Do you track manager satisfaction with recruitment and hiring? If so, how do you do so, and what results have you found?

13. What additional hiring or compensation flexibilities does your organization/agency need, and will you be requesting this additional authority?
14. Is the union workforce covered by the Demo? Were there issues associated with union bargaining? If so, what were they?
15. Does the Demo Project or APS have points of conflict with other parts of your agency due to differing authorities or compensation levels?
16. Can you provide us your 2017 agency/component results for FEVS Q21 (% positive; % negative)?

Bibliography

45 Federal Register 26504, U.S. Office of Personnel Management, Proposed Demonstration Project: An Integrated Approach to Pay, Performance Appraisal, and Position Classification for More Effective Operation of Government Organizations, April 18, 1980.

52 Federal Register 37096, U.S. Office of Personnel Management, Personnel Demonstration Project, Alternative Personnel Management System at the National Bureau of Standards, October 2, 1987.

54 Federal Register 35135, U.S. Office of Personnel Management, Proposed Demonstration Project, Department of Agriculture, August 23, 1989.

55 Federal Register 9062, U.S. Office of Personnel Management, Department of Agriculture, Alternative Personnel Management System Demonstration Project, March 9, 1990.

62 Federal Register 64050, U.S. Office of Personnel Management, Science and Technology Reinvention Laboratory Personnel Demonstration Project at the Naval Sea Systems Command Warfare Centers, December 3, 1997.

62 Federal Register 67434, U.S. Office of Personnel Management, Personnel Demonstration Project, Alternative Personnel Management System for the U.S. Department of Commerce, December 24, 1997.

64 Federal Register 1426, U.S. Department of Defense; Civilian Acquisition Workforce Personnel Demonstration Project, January 8, 1999.

77 Federal Register 48128, National Institute of Standards and Technology, Alternative Personnel Management System (APMS) at the National Institute of Standards and Technology, August 13, 2012.

82 Federal Register 1688, Department of Commerce, Commerce Alternative Personnel System, January 6, 2017.

82 Federal Register 52104, Department of Defense, Civilian Acquisition Workforce Personnel Demonstration (AcqDemo) Project, November 9, 2017.

Alcohol and Tobacco Tax and Trade Bureau, *FY 2014 President's Budget*, Washington, D.C.: Alcohol and Tobacco Tax and Trade Bureau, 2014.

Ban, Carolyn, "QED: The Research and Demonstration Provisions of the Civil Service Reform Act," *Policy Studies Journal*, Vol. 17, No. 2, Winter 1988–1989, pp. 420–434.

Booz Allen Hamilton, *Department of Commerce Personnel Management Demonstration Project Evaluation Year Nine Report*, McLean, Va.: Booz Allen Hamilton, April 15, 2008.

Breul, Jonathan, John Palguta, and Nancy Potok, *Federal Aviation Administration: Personnel Reform Effectiveness Assessment*, Washington, D.C.: National Academy of Public Administration, January 2017.

Cappelli, Peter, "Why We Love to Hate HR . . . and What HR Can Do About It," *Harvard Business Review*, July–August 2015, pp. 54–61. As of March 14, 2019: https://hbr.org/2015/07/why-we-love-to-hate-hr-and-what-hr-can-do-about-it

C.F.R.—*See* Code of Federal Regulations.

Code of Federal Regulations, Title 5, Part 316, Temporary and Term Employment, September 13, 1994

Code of Federal Regulations, Title 5, Part 330, Recruitment, Selection and Placement, August 14, 1971

Code of Federal Regulations, Title 5, Part 332.402, Referring Candidates for Appointment, February 15, 2002

Code of Federal Regulations, Title 5, Part 337, Examining Systems, March 20, 2007

Code of Federal Regulations, Title 5, Part 470.301, Program Expectations, January 21, 1983

Code of Federal Regulations, Title 5, Part 731, Suitability, April 15, 2008.

Cole, William Todd, *Evaluation of the Legacy Science and Technology Reinvention Laboratories*, Washington, D.C.: Defense Civilian Personnel Advisory Service, 2012.

Compassion Capital Fund National Resource Center, *Identifying and Promoting Effective Practices*, Washington, D.C.: Compassion Capital Fund National Resource Center, undated.

Cronk, Terry Moon, "DoD Announces New-Hire Probationary Period," October 3, 2016, U.S. Department of Defense. As of August 8, 2019: https://dod.defense.gov/News/Article/Article/961606/dod-announces-new-hire-probationary-period/

DCIPS—*See* Defense Civilian Intelligence Personnel System.

Defense Civilian Intelligence Personnel System, "About DCIPS," webpage, undated. As of March 20, 2019:
http://www.dami.army.pentagon.mil/site/dcips/about.aspx

———, "Frequently Asked Questions," webpage, updated April 22, 2011. As of March 14, 2019:
https://dcips.defense.gov/Frequently-Asked-Questions/

Defense Civilian Personnel Advisory Service, *The Suitability Guide for Employees*, Washington, D.C.: Defense Civilian Personnel Advisory Service, undated. As of March 14, 2019:
https://www.dcpas.osd.mil/content/Documents/ler/SuitabilityPolicy/suit_guide_for_employees.pdf

———, *Cyber Excepted Service: Frequently Asked Questions*, Washington, D.C.: Defense Civilian Personnel Advisory Service, January 2018. As of March 20, 2019:
https://www.dcpas.osd.mil/content/documents/CyberOneStop/CES/GeneralCESFAQs.pdf

DoD—*See* U.S. Department of Defense

Dorn, Edwin, Dan G. Blair, Diane M. Disney, Martin C. Faga, Kip Hawley, Leo Hazlewood, Janice Lachance, and Michael G. Massiah, *The Defense Civilian Intelligence Personnel System: An Independent Assessment of Design, Implementation, and Impact*, Washington, D.C.: National Academy of Public Administration, June 2010. As of March 14, 2019:
https://www.napawash.org/uploads/Academy_Studies/FINAL-DCIPS-REPORT-June-2010.pdf

Federal Soup, "NSPS—National Security Personnel System," webpage, undated. As of March 14, 2019:
https://forum.federalsoup.com/default.aspx?g=posts&m=124016#post124016

Federal Soup, "TSA Pact Scraps Pay-For-Performance System, webpage, August 10, 2012. As of October 1, 2019:
https://federalsoup.com/articles/2012/08/10/pay-for-performance-system-scrapped-in-tsa-pact.aspx

GAO—*See* U.S. Government Accountability Office.

Ginsberg, Wendy R., *Pay-for-Performance: Lessons from the National Security Personnel System*, Washington, D.C.: Congressional Research Service, RL34673, December 18, 2009.

HireVue, "How to Take a HireVue Interview," webpage, October 7, 2014. As of March 14, 2019:
https://www.hirevue.com/blog/how-to-take-a-hirevue-interview

"The History of Civil Service Reform," in George T. Milkovich and Alexandra K. Wigdor, eds., *Pay for Performance: Evaluating Performance Appraisal and Merit Pay*, Washington, D.C.: National Academies Press, 1991.

Improving Performance: A Review of Pay-for-Performance Systems in the Federal Government: Hearing Before the Subcommittee on Oversight of Government Management, the Federal Workforce, and the District of Columbia, 110 Cong. 814 (2009) (Statement of Ronald Sanders).

Intelligence Community Directive No. 650, *National Civilian Compensation Program: Guiding Principles and Framework*, Washington, D.C.: Officer of the Director of National Intelligence, April 28, 2008.

Katz, Eric, "How Attempts at Fixing the Civil Service System Have Made It Worse Off," *Government Executive*, October 10, 2018. As of March 14, 2019: https://www.govexec.com/management/2018/10/how-attempts-fixing-civil-service -system-have-made-it-worse/151924/

Lamping Lewis, Jennifer, Laura Werber, Cameron Wright, Irina Danescu, Jessica Hwang, and Lindsay Daugherty, *2016 Assessment of the Civilian Acquisition Workforce Personnel Demonstration Project*, Santa Monica, Calif.: RAND Corporation, RR-1783-OSD, 2016. As of September 5, 2019: https://www.rand.org/pubs/research_reports/RR1783.html

"Marking 40 Years with the Civil Service Reform Act," U.S. Government Accountability Office WatchBlog, November 19, 2018. As of March 14, 2019: https://blog.gao.gov/2018/11/19/marking-40-years-with-the-civil-service-reform -act/

National Geospatial-Intelligence Agency, "Compensation," webpage, undated. As of March 14, 2019: https://www.nga.mil/Careers/Benefits/Pages/Compensation.aspx

Neal, Jeff, "Why Hiring Reforms in the 2019 NDAA May Not Make a Difference," FedSmith.com, August 16, 2018. As of March 20, 2019: https://www.fedsmith.com/2018/08/16/ hiring-reforms-2019-ndaa-may-not-make-difference

NDAA—*See* National Defense Authorization Act.

NGA—*See* National Geospatial-Intelligence Agency.

NIST—*See* National Institute of Standards and Technology.

"Notice: Civilian Acquisition Workforce Personnel Demonstration (AcqDemo) Project," Federal Register, Vol. 82, No. 216, November 9, 2017.

OPM—*See* U.S. Office of Personnel Management.

PMA—*See* President's Management Agenda.

Powell, Walter W., and Kaisa Snellman, "The Knowledge Economy," *Annual Review of Sociology*, Vol. 30, August 11, 2004, pp. 199–220.

President's Management Agenda, "Workforce for the 21st Century," webpage, undated. As of September 6, 2019:
https://www.performance.gov/CAP/action_plans/FY2018_Q4_People_Workforce _for_the_21st_Century.pdf

Public Law 86-36, National Security Agency Act of 1959, May 29, 1959.

Public Law 96-191, General Accounting Office Personnel Act of 1980, February 15, 1980.

Public Law 99-574, National Bureau of Standards Authorization Act for Fiscal Year 1987, October 28, 1986.

Public Law 103-282, Title III, Subtitle E, Civilian Employees, NDAA FY 1995, Section 342(b), Extension and Expansion of Authority to Conduct Personnel Demonstration Projects, October 5, 1994.

Public Law 103-337, National Defense Authorization Act for Fiscal Year 1995, October 5, 1994.

Public Law 103-337, National Defense Authorization Act for Fiscal Year 1995, Title III, Subtitle C, Section 342, Extension and Expansion of Authority to Conduct Personnel Demonstration Projects, October 5, 1994.

Public Law 103-337, National Defense Authorization Act for Fiscal Year 1995, Title III, Subtitle E, Civilian Employees, Section 342(b), Defense Laboratories Personnel Demonstration Projects, October 5, 1994.

Public Law 104-113, National Technology Transfer and Advancement Act of 1995, Section 10, Personnel, March 7, 1996.

Public Law 105-206, Internal Revenue Service Restructuring and Reform Act of 1998, July 22, 1998.

Public Law 107-71, Aviation and Transportation Security Act, November 19, 2001.

Public Law 107-296, Homeland Security Act of 2002, November 25, 2002.

Public Law 111-84, National Defense Authorization Act for Fiscal Year 2010, October 28, 2009.

Public Law 114-92, National Defense Authorization Act for Fiscal Year 2016, November 25, 2015.

Public Law 114-190, Title II, Subtitle A, Safety, Section 2106, Hiring of Air Traffic Controllers, July 15, 2016.

Public Law 114-328, Title XI, Subtitle B, Department of Defense Science and Technology Laboratories and Related Matters, Section 1124, Pilot Program on Enhanced Pay Authority for Certain Research and Technology Positions in the Science and Technology Reinvention Laboratories of the Department of Defense, December 23, 2016.

Public Law 115-91, Title IV, Part II, Subtitle E, Section 549, Pilot Programs on Appointment in the Excepted Service in the Department of Defense of Physically Disqualified Former Cadets and Midshipmen, December 12, 2017.

Public Law 115-91, Title VIII, Subtitle D, Provisions Relating to Acquisition Workforce, Section 844, Extension and Modifications to Acquisition Demonstration Project, December 12, 2017.

Public Law 115-91, Title XI, Section 1110, Pilot Program on Enhanced Personnel Management System for Cybersecurity and Legal Professionals in the Department of Defense, December 12, 2017.

Public Law 115-232, John S. McCain National Defense Authorization Act for Fiscal Year 2019, August 13, 2018.

Rein, Lisa, "As Federal Government Evolves, Its Clerical Workers Edge Toward Extinction," *Washington Post*, January 14, 2014. As of March 20, 2019: https://www.washingtonpost.com/politics/as-federal-government-evolves-its -clerical-workers-edge-toward-extinction/2014/01/14/ded78036-5eae-11e3-be07 -006c776266ed_story.html?noredirect=on

Schay, Brigitte W., Research and Demonstration Staff, *Navy Personnel Management Demonstration Project: The Effects of Performance Based Pay on Employee Attitudes*, Washington, D.C.: U.S. Office of Personnel Management, Management Report IV, June 1985.

Slavet, Beth S., Barbara J. Sapin, Susanne T. Marshall, John M. Palguta, Jamie J. Carlyle, Karen K. Gard, and Harry C. Redd III, *The U.S. Office of Personnel Management in Retrospect: Achievements and Challenges After Two Decades*, Washington, D.C.: U.S. Merit Systems Protection Board Office of Policy and Evaluation, December 2001.

Thompson, James R., *Designing and Implementing Performance-Oriented Payband Systems*, Washington, D.C.: IBM Center for the Business of Government, 2007.

———, "Personnel Demonstration Projects and Human Resource Management Innovation," *Review of Public Personnel Administration*, Vol. 28, No. 3, 2008, pp. 240–262. As of March 14, 2019: https://doi.org/10.1177%2F0734371X08318941

Transportation Security Administration, *The Transportation Security Administration's Report to Congress on the Implementation of the Performance Accountability and Standards System (PASS) for the 2007 Performance Cycle*, Washington, D.C.: Transportation Security Administration, May 2008.

Transportation Security Administration Management Directive No. 1100.73-4, Reasonable Accommodation Program, Washington, D.C.: Transportation Security Administration, September 3, 2018.

Treasury Inspector General for Tax Administration, *Some Managerial Salaries Were Calculated Incorrectly Due to Complex Pay-Setting Rules*, Washington, D.C.: Treasury Inspector General for Tax Administration, 2017-10-023, March 29, 2017.

TSA—*See* Transportation Security Administration.

U.S. Code, Title 5, Chapter 47, Personnel Research Programs and Demonstration Projects, January 3, 2012.

U.S. Code, Title 5, Chapter 47, Section 4702, Research Programs, January 3, 2012.

U.S. Code, Title 5, Chapter 47, Section 4703 (b)(1)(H), Demonstration Projects, January 3, 2012.

U.S. Code, Title 5, Chapter 47, Section 4702 (f), Demonstration Projects, January 12, 2018.

U.S. Code, Title 5, Section 4701, Definitions, January 7, 2011.

U.S. Code, Title 5, Section 4703, Demonstration Projects, August 13, 2018.

U.S. Code, Title 10, Chapter 81, Civilian Employees, Section 1599e, Probationary Period for Employees, November 25, 2015.

U.S. Code, Title 10, Chapter 81, Civilian Employees, Section 1599f, Probationary Period for Employees, November 25, 2015.

U.S. Department of Commerce, "Personnel Demonstration Project," Washington, D.C.: U.S. Department of Commerce.

U.S. Department of Commerce, Office of Human Resource Management, "Commerce Alternative Personnel System (CAPS)," webpage, undated. As of January 29, 2018:
https://hr.commerce.gov/Practitioners/CompensationAndLeave/DEV01_006181

U.S. Department of Defense, *An Employee's Guide to CCAS: Understanding the Contribution-Based Compensation and Appraisal System of the DoD Civilian Workforce Personnel Demonstration Project*, Washington, D.C.: U.S. Department of Defense, 2018. As of March 14, 2019:
http://acqdemo.hci.mil/docs/Employee_Guide_to_CCAS_FY18.pdf

U.S. Government Accountability Office, *Federal Personnel: Status of Personnel Research and Demonstration Projects*, Washington, D.C.: U.S. Government Accountability Office, GGD-87-116BR, September 1987.

———, *Federal Personnel: Observations on the Navy's Personnel Management Demonstration Project*, Washington, D.C.: U.S. Government Accountability Office, GGD-88-79, May 3, 1988.

———, *Human Capital Flexibilities*, Washington, D.C.: U.S. Government Accountability Office, GAO-02-1050R, August 9, 2002a. As of March 20, 2019:
https://www.gao.gov/assets/100/91480.pdf

———, *Human Capital: Effective Use of Flexibilities Can Assist Agencies in Managing Their Workforces*, Washington, D.C.: U.S. Government Accountability Office, GAO-03-2, December 6, 2002b.

———, *Financial Regulators—Agencies Have Implemented Key Performance Management Practices, but Opportunities for Improvement Exist*, Washington, D.C.: U.S. Government Accountability Office, GAO-07-678, June 2007.

———, *Final Report on GAO's Use of Provisions in the GAO Human Capital Reform Act of 2004*, Washington, D.C.: U.S. Government Accountability Office, GAO-10-811SP, July 6, 2010. As of March 20, 2019:
https://www.gao.gov/assets/210/204146.pdf

———, *Federal Hiring: OPM Needs to Improve Management and Oversight of Hiring Authorities*, Washington, D.C.: U.S. Government Accountability Office, GAO-16-521, August 2016. As of March 14, 2019:
https://www.gao.gov/assets/680/678814.pdf

———, *Further Actions Needed to Strengthen Oversight and Coordination of Defense Laboratories' Hiring Efforts*, Washington, D.C.: GAO-18-417, May 2018.

U.S. Office of Management and Budget, *The President's Management Agenda*, Washington, D.C.: U.S. Office of Management and Budget, 2002. As of March 14, 2019:
https://georgewbush-whitehouse.archives.gov/omb/budget/fy2002/mgmt.pdf

———, *President's Management Agenda: Modernizing Government for the 21st Century*, Washington, D.C.: U.S. Office of Management and Budget, March 20, 2018. As of March 14, 2019:
https://www.whitehouse.gov/wp-content/uploads/2018/03/Presidents-Management-Agenda.pdf

U.S. Office of Personnel Management, "Hiring Information: Direct Hire Authority," webpage, undated. As of March 20, 2019:
https://www.opm.gov/policy-data-oversight/hiring-information/direct-hire-authority/

———, *Demonstration Projects: Evaluation Handbook*, Washington, D.C.: U.S. Office of Personnel Management, April 1, 1999.

———, *Alternative Personnel Systems in the Federal Government: A Status Report on Demonstration Projects and Other Performance-Based Pay Systems*, Washington, D.C.: U.S. Office of Personnel Management, December 2007. As of March 14, 2019:
https://apps.dtic.mil/dtic/tr/fulltext/u2/a476623.pdf

———, "Historical Federal Workforce Tables: Executive Branch Civilian Employment Since 1940," webpage, 2014. As of March 14, 2019:
https://www.opm.gov/policy-data-oversight/data-analysis-documentation/federal-employment-reports/historical-tables/executive-branch-civilian-employment-since-1940/

———, *End to End Hiring Initiative*, Washington, D.C.: U.S. Office of Personnel Management, March 2017a. As of March 14, 2019:
https://www.opm.gov/policy-data-oversight/human-capital-management/hiring-reform/reference/end-to-end-hiring-initiative.pdf

———, *Federal Employee Viewpoint Survey: Governmentwide Management Report*, Washington, D.C.: U.S. Office of Personnel Management, 2017b. As of March 14, 2019:
https://www.opm.gov/fevs/archive/2017FILES/2017_FEVS_Gwide_Final_Report.PDF

———, *Federal Employee Viewpoint Survey: Governmentwide Management Report*, Washington, D.C.: U.S. Office of Personnel Management, 2018. As of September 6, 2019:
https://www.opm.gov/fevs/reports/governmentwide-reports/governmentwide-management-report/governmentwide-report/2018/2018-governmentwide-management-report.pdf

———, "Personnel Demonstration Project; Pay Banding and Performance-Based Pay Adjustments with the National Nuclear Security Administration," *Federal Register*, Vol. 72, No. 245, December 21, 2007, pp. 72776–72802

———, "Proposed Demonstration Project: An Integrated Approach to Pay, Performance Appraisal, and Position Classification for More Effective Operation of Government Organizations," *Federal Register*, Vol. 45, No. 77, April 18, 1980, pp. 26504–26544

U.S.C.—*See* U.S. Code.

Weichert, Margaret, "OPM Celebrates 40th Anniversary of Civil Service Reform Act," Our Director: U.S. Office of Personnel Management Director's Blog, October 12, 2018. As of March 14, 2019:
https://www.opm.gov/blogs/Director/2018/10/12/OPM-Celebrates-40th-Anniversary-of-Civil-Service-Reform-Act/

Werber, Laura, Lindsay Daugherty, Edward G. Keating, and Matthew Hoover, *An Assessment of the Civilian Workforce Personnel Demonstration Project*, Santa Monica, Calif.: RAND Corporation, TR-1286-OSD, 2012. As of September 5, 2019:
https://www.rand.org/pubs/technical_reports/TR1286.html

Williams, Michelle, Laboratory Quality Enhancement Program Personnel Subpanel Chair, STRL Update Briefing, May 13, 2016.

Wright-Patterson Air Force Base, "AFRL—Air Force Laboratory Personnel Demonstration Project," webpage, July 8, 2016. As of March 14, 2019:
https://www.wpafb.af.mil/Welcome/Fact-Sheets/Display/Article/831901/afrl-air-force-laboratory-personnel-demonstration-project/